Understand

ASSESSME
PRIMARY EDUCATION

Education at SAGE

SAGE is a leading international publisher of journals, books, and electronic media for academic, educational, and professional markets.

Our education publishing includes:

- accessible and comprehensive texts for aspiring education professionals and practitioners looking to further their careers through continuing professional development

- inspirational advice and guidance for the classroom

- authoritative state of the art reference from the leading authors in the field.

Find out more at: **www.sagepub.co.uk/education**

Understanding
ASSESSMENT IN
PRIMARY EDUCATION

SUE FARAGHER

Los Angeles | London | New Delhi
Singapore | Washington DC

Los Angeles | London | New Delhi
Singapore | Washington DC

SAGE Publications Ltd
1 Oliver's Yard
55 City Road
London EC1Y 1SP

SAGE Publications Inc.
2455 Teller Road
Thousand Oaks, California 91320

SAGE Publications India Pvt Ltd
B 1/I 1 Mohan Cooperative Industrial Area
Mathura Road
New Delhi 110 044

SAGE Publications Asia-Pacific Pte Ltd
3 Church Street
#10-04 Samsung Hub
Singapore 049483

Commissioning editor: James Clark
Assistant editor: Rachael Plant
Project manager: Jeanette Graham
Production editor: Thea Watson
Copyeditor: Sharon Cawood
Proofreader: Isabel Kirkwood
Indexer: Anne Solomito
Marketing executive: Dilhara Attygalle
Cover designer: Naomi Robinson
Typeset by: C&M Digitals (P) Ltd, Chennai, India
Printed in India by Replika Press Pvt Ltd

© Sue Faragher 2014

First published 2014

Library of Congress Control Number: 2013957810

British Library Cataloguing in Publication data

A catalogue record for this book is available from
the British Library

ISBN 978-1-4462-7385-2
ISBN 978-1-4462-7386-9 (pbk)

MIX
Paper from
responsible sources
FSC
www.fsc.org FSC® C016779

At SAGE we take sustainability seriously. Most of our products are printed in the UK using FSC papers and boards.
When we print overseas we ensure sustainable papers are used as measured by the Egmont grading system.
We undertake an annual audit to monitor our sustainability.

I would like to dedicate this book to my three wonderful children, Dianne, Steven and Katherine and beautiful granddaughter, Charlotte Sofia.

CONTENTS

LIST OF FIGURES

ABOUT THE AUTHOR

Sue Faragher, EdD, is Headteacher of a large private Primary School in Abu Dhabi. She was formerly a principal lecturer at Liverpool John Moores University and head of the primary and early years programmes. She gained her BEd from Liverpool University followed by a Master's degree from Lancaster University and, finally, a Doctorate from Liverpool John Moores University. She spent many years as a primary school teacher during which time she was awarded Advanced Skills Teacher status. Sue then gained the National Professional Qualification for head teachers prior to becoming a primary head teacher. Following this, she was Advisory Teacher for Assessment before finally moving into Higher Education in 2007 where, in summer 2013, she gained Senior Fellowship of the Higher Education Academy.

ACKNOWLEDGEMENTS

SAGE would like to thank the following reviewers whose comments helped shape the proposal for this book:

Julia Holden – Leeds Trinity University

Rob Morgan – University of Greenwich

Marnie Seymour – University of Winchester

Catherine Thornhill – University of Bedfordshire

Terry Whyte – Canterbury Christ Church University

INTRODUCTION

This book is a practical guide to assessment in primary school, offering key principles and suggesting practical examples of how to use a range of assessment types to monitor the achievements of pupils and identify areas for development. Each chapter includes points for reflection which draw out the main points of the chapter and suggestions for further reading, and there is a full reference list at the end of the book.

Chapter 1 discusses the main principles of assessment and its importance for the pupil, teacher, school and government. It discusses the different forms of assessment, such as formal and informal, continuous and end task, practical, diagnostic and written. It also considers the validity and reliability of tests and highlights the link between motivation and testing.

Chapter 2 considers national and international assessments and the development of these over the past 60 years. It will track the rise of the nation's accountability and standards culture and how this has an increasing focus on an assessment-laden primary curriculum. It will discuss the introduction of international testing and the significance of this within the English economy. It will also explore the reliability and validity of internal and external assessments, including the importance these place on school accountability in the globalised educational world of the twenty-first century. It will examine the shift in emphasis from a bottom-up to a top-down approach to assessment as education policy is increasingly linked to the economy.

Chapter 3 examines the principles of assessing the progress of pupils in early years (EY) and primary schooling, including the role of parents in this process. It offers ways in early years settings and primary schools in which summative assessment can be used formatively and provides a generic format for an assessment grid that can be used to assess the progress of pupils. The chapter also looks at assessment in the early years. This is based on observations of children's learning and development (Drake, 2005). There is also discussion relating to Reading by Six, a phonics-based test aimed at pupils aged 6 which was borne out of research resulting in the publication: *Reading by Six: How the Best Schools Do It* (DfE, 2010a). This based its evidence on a sample of 12 schools which adopt a very rigorous and sequential approach to developing speaking and listening and to the teaching of reading, writing and spelling through systematic phonics.

Chapter 4 considers different ways in which to assess pupils with special educational needs (SEN); this is particularly important as numerous reports indicate that there is poor monitoring of SEN pupils' outcomes. It also considers the use of P scales to measure the progress of pupils with SEN. P scales are a set of descriptions for recording the achievement of pupils with SEN who are working towards the first level of the National Curriculum (level 1) (QCA, 2001). P scales exist for all National Curriculum subjects, and for Personal, Social and Health Education (PSHE) and Citizenship, and Religious Education (RE) although P levels for RE are non-statutory.

Chapter 5 explores the introduction and development of learning through assessment which was first introduced in the 1990s when the government commissioned the Assessment Reform Group to investigate the effectiveness of assessment in primary and secondary schools. The role of this group was to ensure that assessment policy and practice at all levels took account of relevant research evidence. The group concluded that formative assessment could improve learning and published *Inside the Black Box* (Black and Wiliam, 1998). *Assessment for Learning: 10 Principles* (Assessment Reform Group, 2002a), which summarises the key features that resulted from extensive research into Assessment for Learning, outlines the ten principles that lead to changing assessment practice in the classroom, whilst at the same time maintaining the quality of learning experiences. Assessment for Learning (AfL) is a natural, integral and essential part of everyday learning and teaching and a key element of personalised learning. Teachers and pupils continually reflect on how learning is progressing and where improvements can be made, and identify the next steps to take to achieve goals. The primary and secondary Assessment for Learning National Strategies both offer key support in developing the different strands within the classroom. The Office for Standards in Education (Ofsted, 2008a), however, indicated that AfL was no better than satisfactory in more than two thirds of schools visited, although it was better developed in primary than secondary schools.

Chapter 6 explains the purposes and principles of peer and self-assessment. It investigates the advantages and disadvantages of these and offers practical ways in which assessment strategies can be introduced to pupils. It also considers research that investigates how pupil and teacher assessment compares with self-assessment.

Self-assessment is the process of looking at oneself and assessing set aspects of learning or making judgements about an aspect of performance. Its advantage is that it self-motivates the pupil to enhance their learning, whilst a disadvantage is that it may affect self-esteem and self-efficacy. Therefore, it is essential that self-assessment is taught and linked directly with the learning outcomes and success criteria of the session. Self-assessment can be successful in other areas such as behaviour skills and character, in addition to the curriculum subjects; it can be personalised and is a means by which pupils have an increased role in their learning and begin to work at a metacognitive level. The essence of self-assessment is to reflect on why things went wrong and develop a way to improve, rather than apportioning blame for what went wrong.

Peer assessment complements self-assessment and usually employs the same principles although peer assessment is making judgements on other pupils' learning and/or performance rather than one's own. In many cases, peer assessment is valuable. Clarke's (2001) research supports the fact that pupils often accept criticism more readily from peers than from the teacher. It is also valuable in the interchange of shared understanding of the language used between peers and the learning that takes place between teacher and pupil. Additionally, pupils are more likely to interrupt a peer than a teacher if they do not fully understand a comment or aspect of the learning. It also offers an opportunity for the teacher to observe the interactions and interject as appropriate.

The chapter also examines the fact that peer feedback, involving the spoken or written word, as opposed to providing a grade, is much more effective in promoting future learning. However, as with self-assessment, peer assessment needs to be linked closely to the learning objectives and success criteria of the session and specifically taught so that pupils understand the type of comments they should give to assess their peers and promote future learning.

The next four chapters consider ways in which to assess pupils that don't involve paper tests or worksheets, and the advantages and disadvantages of such methods. It provides practical examples of how these strategies may be adopted in the classroom.

Chapter 7 highlights the ethical issues in using observations as an assessment method. Is it ethical to observe and assess a pupil if he/she is unaware it is happening? Alternatively, if he/she were told, would it affect or change their behaviour, achievement or competence? There are therefore both overt and covert methods of observation which can be typified by five techniques: participant and non-participant observation, structured and unstructured observation and naturalistic observation. In Foundation 1 and 2 classrooms in which pupils aged 3–5 learn, and in the medical profession, assessment is largely through observations and it is from this literature that one can draw advantages and disadvantages and useful strategies and tactics to employ for maximum effect. Observation is a practical research tool that provides a wealth of information on knowledge, skills and behaviours which provides insight into pupils' progress, learning, abilities and areas for development. Additionally, there is a range of recording techniques, from learning journeys to digital methods, which is also discussed in this chapter.

Mind maps are visual diagrams used to pictorially represent information (D'Antoni, 2006). They are often created around a word or phrase placed in the centre of the page with associated ideas, words, phrases or concepts around it. Sub-branches may be added as appropriate. Diagrams that map information can be traced back to the 3rd century, although their modern-day popularity was reinstated by psychologist and mathematician, Tony Buzan, in the 1970s.

Mind mapping is a useful technique in the classroom for learning new information, recording thoughts and ideas and enhancing creative problem solving. The power of mind maps lies in the way in which they represent how pupils think, with ideas instantly classified and grouped as they arise (D'Antoni et al., 2010). It can also be practised in any subject, with any language and with most pupils in primary school. Mento et al. (1999) supports the fact that mind mapping taps into your whole brain, thus releasing the brain's potential with less work for the memory. Therefore, a mind map is a hierarchical structure that connects imagination with structures and pictures with logic and is a dynamic tool to ensure thinking and planning become a more efficient process. Within the classroom, mind maps can be used at the beginning, in the middle or at the end of a lesson or topic, in order to assess the knowledge and understanding of the pupils.

Chapter 8 explores the concept of asking questions which is natural and intuitive and has a long history as an educational strategy – very often drawing citations from Socrates. Historically, teachers have asked questions to check what has been learnt, to gauge whether to move forward or to revise or assess. Nevertheless, as a strategy it can be used to challenge assumptions, expose contradictions and lead to new learning. Wragg (2001) suggests that questioning by teachers is widespread with anywhere between 35 and 50 per cent of the time spent on questioning. However, this chapter focuses on using questioning as a constructive, active strategy through the use of higher-order thinking, questioning and explanatory skills, in order to develop enquiring minds through the use of Bloom's taxonomy. Additionally, a teacher who models effective questioning can encourage this to extend to pupils' home life too.

Debates have been used in many professions to present a thought-provoking teaching tool that focuses on self-learning. Planning debates can also help organise thoughts and reinforce ideas. Debates can be used to teach difficult or controversial topics and can improve learning and critical thinking, and develop reasoning and communication skills. Debates also transfer the pupil from being a passive to an active learner and can be beneficial when analysing, testing and evaluating arguments. Debating activities in schools can contribute not only to educational achievement but to wider skills that work towards developing more confident and well-rounded individuals.

Chapter 9 discusses the use of reports, role play and portfolios as alternative forms of assessment. It is important to understand that assessment data can be generated in many different ways, many of which require little or no written work. This chapter explains the ways in which data on pupil learning can be gathered through different sources. Verbal or written reports are one way in which cognitive data can be collected for assessment purposes. One difficulty may be in deciding whether the report should be open-ended and unstructured or structured with a defined reporting style. A more structured report offers the most reliability and validity of pupil understanding and progress in learning, although reports in general can be adopted as an assessment tool in most subjects of the curriculum.

Role play can be described as a range of activities characterised by involving pupils in simulated conditions or roles. Role play may range from minimalist settings and short duration to highly complex extended situations. It is a way to deliberately create aspects of real life under controlled conditions. It can be used to illustrate a range of feelings, create empathy or explore the social nature of learning. It can generate enthusiasm in a topic, help pupils become active learners, involving them directly in their learning, and teach pupils to understand the different perspectives of peers or different cultures or peoples in history.

The use of portfolios as an assessment tool can develop pupils' cognitive and metacognitive abilities (Hebert, 2001). Portfolios concentrate on the thinking and understanding rather than the end product. A portfolio details what has been learnt, how it has been learnt and the thinking–analysing–synthesising process. It enhances thinking about thinking and enhances learning, as usually the pupil is unaware of their internal thinking process.

Chapter 10 examines the use of information and communication technology (ICT) in assessment. There are issues of validity, efficiency, type of response and means of scoring when using ICT in assessment, as scores are not formative feedback and cannot therefore be used to promote further learning. It is important to understand what is being assessed and how it relates to the teaching. Progress tracking that measures achievement is perhaps the most popular form of ICT in assessment.

However, moving away from summative electronic assessments, ICT can be used formatively as an assessment tool in a variety of ways – for example, assessing ICT skills, for combining ICT and geography skills through the production of an informative poster, researching the internet to complete an assessment on the water cycle or developing a concept map on the learning of life in Tudor times. Additionally, there is a range of electronic educational games that assess mathematics (or maths), creativity, the use of English, and so on. This chapter will also consider the use of ICT in a wider context through the use of digital cameras, video, clickers, PDAs, Roamers, etc., to assess pupils' learning. Finally, the chapter looks at the difficulties and disadvantages of using ICT in assessment, from electronic failure to gender differences in approaching ICT-based assessments.

Chapter 11 examines how feedback and target setting as an assessment strategy promotes learning. It offers different ways in which to record assessments and details the statutory duties relating to assessment, recording and reporting which must be adhered to, including the annual report on the progress of pupils for their parents.

The final chapter will draw together the major points of the preceding chapters, leaving the reader with a clear message about the purpose and uses of assessment in primary school and the merits and drawbacks of using a wide range of different assessment strategies. It will revisit the differences between summative and formative assessment and, finally, discuss the importance of statutory and non-statutory assessment in the accountability culture of the present globalised economy.

CHAPTER 1

INTRODUCTION TO THE PRINCIPLES OF ASSESSMENT

Chapter Objectives

1 To understand the purpose of assessment
2 To understand the differences between formative and summative assessment and their relative uses
3 To understand the many different formats of assessment

In the late 20th century, the aim of the Assessment Reform Group was to ensure that assessment policy and practice took account of relevant research evidence. It published well-known booklets such as *Inside the Black Box* (Black and Wiliam, 1998); *Working Inside the Black Box* (Black et al., 2002) and *Assessment for Learning: Putting It Into Practice* (Black and Wiliam, 2002), all designed to enhance assessment practices in the primary classroom. But despite many research articles and much government documentation since this time, such as Excellence and Enjoyment in the Primary School (2003) and the Primary National Strategy (2011), the National Student and Newly

Qualified Teacher Surveys indicate that assessment is a consistent concern for many trainee teachers and early practitioners in primary schools.

The word *assessment* is often associated with anxiety, fear and formality, as generations of pupils have been subjected to an increasing amount of public examinations. Pupils are tested, schools are inspected and teachers are appraised in a highly accountable education system. Therefore, with a system with an increasing focus on testing and accountability, it is important for primary educators to understand why assessment is important and how best to assess pupils. This book is not an instruction manual but seeks to suggest a variety of ways in which primary pupils can be assessed.

Assessment in primary school is essentially concerned with gathering evidence about what pupils can do, know or understand. It would be easy if there were one assessment that you could administer at some point in primary school that provided all the information needed on pupils' progress, but pupils' knowledge, skills and understanding can be assessed through a range of formal or informal assessments initiated by you as the teacher, or, alternatively, pupils can assess themselves and their peers. In fact, pupils' knowledge and understanding of factual information, theories, concepts and ideas; their mental and physical ability; their attitudes and beliefs about learning, people and society; their behaviour in social relationships, their personal integrity, their fulfilment of their potential and their perseverance and willingness to solve problems are continually assessed in the classroom almost instinctively. This is a skill that develops the more experienced you become as a teacher and is useful for planning activities that will result in pupils' optimum learning.

Additionally, there is a range of statutory assessments for primary pupils, such as the Early Years Foundation Stage Profile (EYFSP) for pupils aged 5, Reading by Six and Key Stage 1 and 2 Standard Attainment Tests (SATs) for pupils aged 7 and 11 respectively. Apart from the Key Stage 2 SATs for pupils aged 11, all tests are marked, analysed and interpreted by teachers. It is therefore important for teachers to be able to use the data produced from such tests to inform the future planning of lesson content.

Assessment can be divided into two broad categories: summative and formative. Both have their purposes and both are important for different reasons. It is also possible to use summative assessments formatively so that pupils' learning may improve from all types of assessment.

Summative assessment

Summative assessment, as it sounds, provides a summary record of a pupil's learning at one point in time. Typically, summative assessments are statutory and the results are disseminated to parents, the local authority and governors or, in the case of the Key Stage 2 SATs, reported nationally and placed in national league tables. Summative results are important throughout a pupil's schooling as they provide parents, teachers, the local authority, the government and the public with an indication of what has been learned and how pupils in one school compare with pupils in other schools. Indeed, without summative assessments how would employers know whether they should take on a pupil to train as a doctor, an engineer or a teacher? Summative tests are also used in some areas of the country to decide the school to which a pupil will transfer at the age of 11. These may be 11+ or entrance exams to assess if a pupil is deemed suitable for that particular primary or secondary school. Primary schools may also administer their own end of topic or end of year tests to assess the learning of pupils.

Many statutory or summative tests are norm-referenced where the time is limited and there is a set content. They can be administered at the end of a unit of work, at the end of a year or at the end of a key stage such as the SATs (for pupils aged 7 and 11) and the EYFSP (for pupils aged 5).

The National Curriculum for ages 5 to 16, first introduced in the 1988 Education Reform Act, brought with it statutory assessment. There have been several changes to National Curriculum tests, most recently in 2012. For early years pupils, statutory curriculum and testing were introduced in the Children's Act 2006 with the EYFS. It became statutory in 2008 and is applicable to pupils from birth to 5 in all pre-schools, nurseries and childcare centres. It is summatively assessed using the EYFSP when pupils are aged 5. The EYFSP, along with the most recent addition to the statutory assessment of pupils in the early years, Reading by Six, will be further explored in Chapter 3.

Formative assessment

Formative assessment is concerned with assessment that identifies where pupils are in their learning, where they need or want to be and how best to bridge that gap (Black and Wiliam, 1998; Cowie and Bell, 1999;

Assessment Reform Group, 2002b). It was first promoted by the Assessment Reform Group which was commissioned in 1990 to gather research evidence on which types of assessment work best. It can include ongoing, almost subconscious, judgements or more formal assessments and is a cyclical process of assessment, evaluation and feedback with suggestions on how pupils can improve. The Primary National Strategy introduced in 2004 promoted the use of formative strategies to enhance the learning of pupils. This was based on various reports, notably those from Black and colleagues (Black and Wiliam, 1998, 2002; Black et al., 2002, 2003a) and the Assessment Reform Group (2002b), and is evidenced in books by Clarke (1998, 2001, 2005a, 2005b, 2008), Gardner (2006) and Pardoe (2009). It includes strategies such as *think-pair-share* and *wait time* – approaches to assessing learning which are explored further in Chapter 5.

Assessment may also be formal or informal. For example, if the government wishes to elicit whether primary pupils' ability to write effectively in a range of genres has improved, a formal test is more practical. However, should a teacher wish to know if pupils understand the safety regulations before handling tools in technology, the assessment would be informal although no less important.

Formal assessment is often more structured, planned and organised. It involves statutory exams or in-school tests which require the assessment to be executed on a particular day in a particular way and within a set timescale. It does not need to be unpleasant, unfriendly or intimidating and can be executed through a range of different kinds of assessments, as evidenced throughout this book. It is merely governed by a set of rules rather than being spontaneous (Wragg, 2001).

In most primary classrooms, assessment is informal and almost continuous throughout the day. As a teacher, you will continually assess whether pupils have understood knowledge, concepts, health and safety regulations and how to behave. You will evaluate the standard of pupils' work, replies and responses to questions or the interaction in group situations and you will then calculate when a pupil is ready to move on in their learning. Teaching is often a dialogue between you and the pupils and you are required to make split-second decisions whilst on the move (Wragg, 2001). You will be unable to reflect on decisions as time demands that you respond quickly to situations that arise in the classroom. It will be evident as you become a more experienced teacher that assessment is barely noticeable in the classroom; rather, it flows seamlessly as you are continually monitoring the situation, addressing pupils' needs and taking their learning to the next level.

The differences between formal and informal testing are clear. Teaching is a busy, demanding profession and informal, frequent assessments are invaluable for identifying where pupils are in their learning, where they need to be and how to get there. Such assessment allows for an understanding of the progress of the whole child in a range of subjects and situations. However, it is subjective and unreflective whereas more formal assessment provides opportunities to see the bigger picture, allowing for a comparison of groups of pupils within the school and against different schools, and is more objective and systematic. Formal assessment, such as multiple-choice questions, may also have other drivers unrelated to pupils' attainment and achievement, such as ease of administration, marking and analysis of the data. But formal assessments may intimidate less confident or less able pupils, affecting their performance, and can only provide a limited picture of learning across a range of subjects over a period of time.

Assessment may also be continuous coursework or a final judgement of achievement through a test or exam. In working life, it is rare to sit an exam but more likely that performance will be measured through a continual process. Continuous assessment is commonly found in secondary school when pupils are working towards a national exam. The course is modular and is assessed as each part is completed. A major concern of modular and continuously assessed work is its validity and integrity. It is open to plagiarism, from the internet and books or other people completing the work in addition to the pupil. Difficulties arise when pupils have been encouraged to seek support from members of their family but the adult does not know how to support their child without providing them with the answers. Media reports, such as *The Times* newspaper report of such abuse (Gilbert, 2012), question the reliability and trustworthiness of the testing system for the licensing of professionals such as teachers.

Within primary school, continuous assessment may take place through topic work or throughout a unit of work. Continuous assessment is thought to be advantageous to pupils who worry about final exams, although gaining repeated feedback that details their need to improve can also cause a pupil to become disheartened and therefore fail to achieve. This of course links closely with motivation and feedback. If motivation is high, then pupils will respond eagerly to suggestions for improvement; alternatively, those with low self-esteem may lose interest and motivation in the unit of study. Regular feedback can affect motivation and self-esteem positively or negatively by either detailing achievable and appropriate ways in which to improve or focusing on what is wrong and fails to reach the expected standard. The importance of feedback is discussed further in Chapter 5.

There are arguments which suggest that final assessment is essential in motivating pupils to work towards a final target, whilst in continuous assessment it may be difficult to see the ultimate goal. Essentially, the discussion between coursework and a final assessment hinges on whether pupils respond well to extrinsic or intrinsic motivation (Wragg, 2001). Pupils who seek to improve the final mark, grade or score, regarding this as the ultimate reward, respond well to extrinsic motivation, whilst those who are concerned with the process of learning itself, with the end test result as a by-product, respond better to intrinsic motivation. Research suggests that extrinsic motivation is short-lived and will need to be reignited for the next task whereas intrinsic motivation self-perpetuates learning (Black and Wiliam, 1998; Black et al., 2003b; Clarke, 2001, 2005a, 2005b, 2008). At present, national tests grade pupils aged 5, 6, 7 and 11 through an end of year test, and pupils aged 16, 17 and 18 by a mixture of continuous course work using a modular system assessment and final examination. Whereas the modular system is somewhat contentious as it allows for multiple retakes of modules, it is a system of non-competitive evaluation and is preferred by pupils who may panic or be anxious at an end of course exam which assesses the learning of the whole programme of work. It could be argued, therefore, that continuous assessment with a final test at the end of the unit of work may be the best option as it satisfies both extrinsic and intrinsic motivation for learning.

It is not always essential that assessments are written or that they focus on the achievement of the individual. Assessments may be oral, written or practical and conducted with individuals or groups of pupils. Of course, some assessments fall naturally into one bracket or another such as art and design, musical or physical assessments. It would be difficult to assess if a pupil were able to play a tune on a flute or perform a back somersault on a trampoline through a written test. Similarly, asking a pupil in the early years to write about their favourite animal would be meaningless as they will not yet have the skills to do this effectively. Alternatively, if the assessment was to ascertain if a pupil could use a range of connections in their writing, this would be difficult to assess through a practical or oral test. Therefore, the subject, the purpose of the assessment, the time limit available, the age of the pupil, the knowledge or skill to be assessed, all need to be considered in deciding which type of assessment will provide the best indication of the pupil's progress.

Often, the type of assessment chosen is decided by the need for evidence to be gathered. If a teacher needs verification that a pupil has achieved a level or skill, then the assessment tends to be written although this need not be lengthy prose but could be a drawing, multiple choice, cloze passages or text on a computer. This may allow pupils to complete the assessment in their own time, although this will depend on the purpose of the assessment. Assessment of course can be done orally but the time taken for each pupil to sit with you as the teacher makes it more appropriate for a written account to be completed. If it is informal and immediate, then it tends to be oral although early years practitioners are expert in the use of observation and recording of evidence to demonstrate a pupil's learning.

Practical tests can be used for different reasons such as offering an alternative way for pupils with speech and communication difficulty, for example, to highlight their understanding. It is also a useful strategy for demonstrating skills such as those in technology, science, music, art and drama. In many cases, practical activities can assess whether the pupil is knowledgeable and can apply the skills operationally. It is also important for you when assessing practical skills to ensure that pupils do not fail to observe vital evidence in their recording of the activity. It is a good idea to plan the observation and reflect on the evidence to ensure it is a true representation of pupils' abilities.

Whether practical, oral or written tests are used, it is inevitable that some pupils will be advantaged over others. The proficient, lucid writer may favour a written test whilst a skilful orator may prefer an oral exam and a pragmatic pupil may wish to engage in a practical test. It is for this reason that it is important to vary the types of assessment throughout the curriculum. Once again, the value of all assessments is in the feedback provided for pupils allowing them to progress in their learning. In all assessments, it is important for you to decide what is to be assessed and recorded, how it will be assessed, the way in which the outcomes of written, oral and practical skills can be moderated and how the results will be fed back to pupils to enhance their learning (Wragg, 2001).

Most formal assessment is individual as it builds up a profile of each pupil in order that judgements can be made at certain times of the pupil's schooling – for example, in order to decide which primary or secondary school to attend, which group or set is best to enhance pupils' learning, what to feed back to parents at parents' evenings. At other times, pupils' work is assessed as a group, such as with a drama performance, a debate, school sports day, a dance performance, science or technology experiments and a group project such as a traffic survey or a report on different aspects of Tudor life. Group assessment may provide you with a difficulty in that there is a dilemma in whether to offer individual marks with which the pupils may disagree or a group grade in which there may have been pupils who worked harder or provided more of the information than others. One solution may be to offer to comment and feed back only on the group dynamics, the way in which pupils worked as a team, the way in which all played a different but important part, with the content and outcome as secondary. Alternatively, pupils may be asked to self- or peer-assess the group activity or performance which hands the responsibility of assessment to the pupils themselves. The type, form and who to assess of course depends on the objectives set for the activity, which should be clearly expressed to pupils prior to beginning the project. Although group work is difficult to assess, it is good grounding for later life and should be practised in primary school, as in adulthood many situations require people to work in teams and groups.

It is also useful for assessments to provide a diagnosis of achievements and areas for development, and therefore it is possible to conduct a diagnostic test or use the data of a previous test to provide information for future teaching sessions. Diagnostic tests, as they suggest, identify strengths and weaknesses in pupils' learning and are commonplace in life, such as driving tests to ascertain competency at driving, blood tests that assess infection, eye exams that test sight and cholesterol tests to see how much fat is contained in the blood. Within education, there are tests for pupils with physical and behavioural disabilities, for pupils with specific learning difficulties and for those with speech, visual or hearing impairment.

But within the normal classroom there are ways in which assessments can be used diagnostically so that the strengths and development needs of pupils are highlighted. At the basic level, every assessment, including marking pupils' work, should include areas of success and ways to improve. This, at a day-to-day level, is formative assessment which is diagnostic.

At a summative level, it seems at first glance that it would be difficult to use this data as diagnostic. However, all assessment has the potential to offer rich information on what was done well and what areas need addressing. For example, the Reading by Six phonic assessments can provide you with valuable information on the ability of pupils to blend, segment, encode and decode words, provided you analyse the results. Even the 20 nonsense words provide an indication as to whether pupils can apply the phonic knowledge they have to new unidentified words. The nonsense words ensure that pupils are using their phonic knowledge rather than recognition of the whole word. Of course, there are many who would argue that learning to read is not just about phonics but about recognising the shapes of words and there are words that cannot be deciphered simply through phonic decoding. Similarly, in the teacher's handbook of the Key Stage 2 English reading test, it indicates the type of each question, such as descriptive, inference, deduction and factual. Should you analyse the scripts when returned, each pupil would have a reading profile of successes and areas for development which could then be passed on to secondary school. It may also have implications for the teaching of pupils aged 10 and 11 in the following year if the class profile indicated that the children were weak on, for example, inferring information from poetry.

Diagnostic assessments are useful for measuring the progress of individuals and classes, identifying areas of misunderstanding or lack of mastery of a skill, analysing errors in reading such as miscue analysis or evaluating the readiness of a pupil, group of pupils or the class to move on to more challenging activities. Diagnostic tests tend to be either norm referenced or criterion referenced.

Norm-referenced diagnostic tests tend to place the pupil on a scale against all other pupils of the same age and focus on the overall mark of a set task. Criterion-referenced diagnostic tests analyse the different components of the assessment and construct a personal profile of the topic, highlighting which aspects of the test have been understood and which need revisiting. Therefore, norm-referenced tests offer an overall figure for comparison across pupils, classes, year groups and schools. Criterion-referenced tests drill down into the profile of each pupil to identify strengths and weaknesses. One of the criticisms of diagnostic testing is that the focus is on areas of weakness rather than on achievements and that sometimes the individual components are lost within the whole. For example, in a reading test, comprehension, fluidity, word recognition, intonation, prediction, phonic knowledge and awareness of punctuation may all be assessed although this would be impossible within one test. Therefore, diagnostic tests need to be specific. Focus on weakness can also be avoided by applying the 3:2 or 2:1 rule. That is, offer three positive points and two areas for development (or two positive points and one area for development) or any combination where the number of positive points outweighs the areas of weakness. This is sometimes referred to as *stars and a wish* – for example, three stars and a wish would mean that three areas of success are highlighted along with one area that needs to be developed.

Validity of assessments

Within all assignments, it is important to consider the validity and reliability of the activity so that it can offer data that is accurate and trustworthy. Validity ensures that the test measures what it sets out to do. As a teacher, you need to have a clear understanding of what is expected of the test. For example, if it is to write up a scientific experiment and the teacher reports on the spelling and sentence structure then that test is invalid. Wragg (2001) suggests that there are four types of validity in assessment: face validity, content validity, concurrent validity and predictive validity.

Face validity is concerned with the face value of assessments and is particularly evident in written questions. The question may be a mathematical computation or knowledge of geographical or historical facts but if written it assumes the pupil has a general understanding of language and what language means. For example, if the questions were – How many wives had Henry VIII? How long was he king? Who succeeded him to the throne? – this is testing not only historical knowledge but language skills (VIII; succeeded) and quite advanced mathematical skills, subtracting 21 April 1509 when Henry came to the throne from 28 January 1547 when he died. Combinations of assessments are fine to use as long as there has been a consideration of the face validity in the design of the questions. Ensure the assessment tests what it intends to test and does not penalise any pupil because of the language or other skills required to answer the focus question.

Content validity requires the assessment to reflect the content of the unit of work being taught. Therefore, the assessment should reflect what has been taught and the time spent on that area. For example, if for two thirds of the term there has been a focus on place value and a third on adding and subtracting decimals, then the assessment task should reflect the same weighting of two thirds/one third. Whereas face value looks at the way in which specific questions are expressed, content validity considers the appropriateness of the weighting of each question depending on the prior teaching.

Concurrent validity refers to the way in which different ways of assessing a pupil give the same result. For example, when explaining the life cycle of a frog, pupils may draw a picture, write an account, explain orally or design a flow chart. All should indicate the same result. It is also evident with the SATs for pupils aged 7 and 11, where you should find that your assessment indicates a similar result to that indicated by the test. Of course, there will be slight variations in this as the teacher often bases their assessment on the pupil over a period of time whereas the SAT measures attainment at a particular time in a particular area of reading, writing, spelling or maths. Another example of concurrent validity would be whether those pupils who write creatively in English can also apply this across the curriculum or are just particularly good writers of stories because they have a lot of experience of stories being read to them in their formative years.

Predictive validity is concerned with assessments that predict the future course of the pupil. This may be to determine which class, set or group the pupil should be in, who should take the lead role in the Christmas play or be selected for the swimming team. You will need to learn to predict the future and select pupils for the most appropriate activity. Predictive validity is best the closer it is to the time and subject matter of the area being tested; pupils should not be labelled early on in their schooling as slow early development is not necessarily a predictor of how the pupil will perform in five, six or ten years' time.

Assessment validity (Johnson, 2012) measures how well the assessment quantifies what it is intended to evaluate. It is concerned with how personal preferences, knowledge, skills and understanding impact on the assessment type used and on the criteria applied in the assessment of pupils' responses. Therefore, the task set and the marking and evaluation of pupils' work must relate to the learning objectives of the lesson.

Reliability of assessment

Reliability ensures that responses are consistent whenever an activity is marked by the same person. But unless the assessment has validity there is little point in considering its reliability. As you will read in Chapter 2, governments seem to focus on the reliability of test results whereas teachers focus on their validity. For example, it is possible, when marking, that on the last ten scripts of the third set of 30 books the teacher may lose a little concentration and mark more erratically than on the first 10 books of the first set of 30. This renders the task unreliable. Similarly, it is possible that marking the same script two days apart may result in different feedback. This is why moderation of work is important across classes, year groups, key stages and the school. It is not to catch teachers out but to ensure pupils have the fairest feedback so that they can progress in their learning. Assessment reliability (Johnson, 2011) is concerned with consistency in that if the original tools for assessment were changed then the same results would emerge. Having said that, it is difficult in some cases to assess pupils' skills and attitudes and it may only be possible to be certain of the results of these when several assessments have been completed.

It is fruitless if the tests are valid and reliable but the subject is irrelevant, dull or boring. It is important therefore to decipher what is worth assessing and recording, to match assessment to purpose and to consider what is feasible in the time and with the resources available.

Finally, the focus of UK governments in the twenty-first century has been on accountability, which requires the school's assessment results to be published in the school prospectus and reports to be sent out to parents, governing bodies, local authorities and the school inspection body, the Office for Standards in Education (Ofsted). Key Stage 2 SATs for pupils aged 11 are also published in league tables and reported in the media. When Ofsted inspectors visit a school, assessment processes, amongst other things, become the focus. The school needs to provide evidence that all pupils, including those with SEN, are progressing at or above the expected rate. Up until 2012, Ofsted inspectors would evaluate value-added scores to ascertain whether all pupils were progressing in their learning. Value-added measures the achievement made from the starting point of entry to school, usually at age 4 or 5, to where the pupil is at the point of inspection. Since 2012, value-added has been removed and the data reports on attainment only. There is no account taken of first language spoken, social and economic deprivation, the number of books in the home or the level of parental support; it is raw data. Assessment may also lead to a self-fulfilling prophecy in that if pupils believe they continually perform below what is expected then they may choose not to engage with the learning for fear of further failure. This, if not remedied, can lead to the pupil being labelled and stereotyped as a reluctant learner. All assessments have outcomes and it is your role to ensure there are neither too many nor too few assessments, adversely affecting pupils in your class. Each assessment should have clear aims and objectives which identify what is to be assessed, how it is to be assessed and the expected outcome of the assessment. Assessment and feedback should be focused on the objectives rather than on the neatness, behaviour or attentiveness to detail of the pupil. It is important to remember that assessments can only test the pupil's knowledge, skills or understanding and therefore the objectives of the assessment are limited. The more focused the assessment is, the more valid and reliable it will be in offering accurate data on each pupil's progress.

Points for Reflection

- Why do we assess pupils?
- What is the difference between formative and summative assessment?
- What is the importance of appropriateness, validity and reliability of tests?
- What different types of assessment do you carry out now? Which will you try out?

Further Reading

The following books and articles will enhance your knowledge and understanding of statutory and non-statutory assessments:

Harlen, W. and Gardner, J. (2006) *On the Relationship Between Assessment for Formative and Summative Purposes*. London: SAGE.

Leung, C. and Mohan, B. (2004) *Teacher Formative Assessment and Talk in Classroom Contexts: Assessment as Discourse and Assessment of Discourse*. London: SAGE.

Tarras, M. (2005) 'Assessment – Summative and Formative – Some Theoretical Reflections', *British Journal of Educational Studies*, 53(4): 466–78.

Torrance, H. and Pryor, J. (2001) 'Developing Formative Assessment in the Classroom: Using Action Research to Explore and Modify Theory', *British Educational Research Journal*, 27(5): 615–31.

Wiliam, D. (2006) 'Formative Assessment: Getting the Focus Right', *Educational Assessment*, 11(3–4): 283–9.

CHAPTER 2

STANDARDS-DRIVEN ASSESSMENT CULTURE

Chapter Objectives

1 To track the development of assessment policy since the 1944 Education Act
2 To understand the changing focus of assessments from a bottom-up to a top-down approach
3 To understand the importance of assessment within a globalised economy

Introduction

This chapter considers both national and international assessments and the development of these over the past 60 years. It tracks the history of the UK's increasing accountability and standards culture (Zajda and Rust, 2009) and indicates how this has an increasing focus on an assessment-laden primary curriculum (Tomlinson, 2005). The reliability and validity of internal and external assessments are examined, including the importance these place on school accountability in the globalised educational world of the twenty-first century (Butt and Lance, 2005; Gunter, 2007), where the emphasis from a bottom-up to a top-down approach to assessment increasingly links to the country's economy.

History of educational testing

Education for All was the main essence of the 1944 Education Act (Butler, 1944) which first proposed that all pupils between the ages of 5 and 15, whatever their aptitude or ability, should be educated in an appropriate primary, secondary grammar, secondary technical or secondary modern school or, alternatively, an institution for those who were *feeble of mind or body* (Education Act 1944). It was the first time that free education had been offered to pupils over the age of 11 and although at this time the government's focus was on regenerating the country post-war, it seemed to recognise that pupils in schools would be the next generation of workers and key to the future success of the economy; the focus was on educating not testing the pupil.

Harold Wilson, the Labour Prime Minister in 1964, anxious to keep the education system pupil-centred, heavily financed the education sector, spending more money on education than defence (Gillard, 2011). Three years later, *Pupils and their Primary Schools* (Plowden, 1967) was published, signalling a time of excitement and positivity in education. The 11+ intelligence test was being abolished, streaming by ability was being abandoned, and pupil-centred approaches, flexibility of the curriculum and an emphasis on personalisation of the teaching and learning process were advocated. Primary school teachers had enormous freedom to experiment with progressive styles of teaching, creativity and spontaneity based wholly on the needs of individual pupils. Testing and assessment of the pupil were not high on the agenda. Tests within schools were used internally to ensure the pupil was taught at the right level to extend learning. However, the autonomy of *Pupils and their Primary Schools* (Plowden, 1967) was short-lived as three years later (1970) the Conservative government heavily criticised the pupil-centred approach and policies promoting education for all, believing that through focusing on the needs of the pupil, education standards were falling.

Consequently, the 1970s initiated the start of central government beginning to take control of education. Educational powers were removed from local education authorities and given to the governing bodies of individual schools, which resulted in schools being given more responsibility, yet being subjected to more control, assessment and evaluation. This was the beginning of the testing and assessment culture that is prevalent today.

Over the next 30 years, education was seen to be the key to economic prosperity; politicians took increasing control of education. In October 1976, James Callaghan, the Labour Prime Minister, condemned the progressive education of the *Pupils and their Primary Schools* report (Plowden, 1967) and indicated that the education system should reflect the economic need for Britain to continue to compete in a highly competitive world. It indicated an increased intervention of central government in education, resulting in a range of increasingly detailed policies and reports such as: the Education Act (1976); the Taylor Report (1977); the Waddell Report (1978) and the Assessment of Performance Unit (2008), all focused on reforming the curriculum and assessing pupils' progress in an effort to increase educational standards.

The Assessment of Performance Unit played an increasing part in defining educational standards and was a powerful influence on the control of English education, requiring that one third of pupils be assessed in key subject areas. It did not focus on individual schools, teachers or local authorities but rather on the teaching profession as a whole. Nevertheless, a survey by Gipps and Goldstein (1983) revealed that most local authorities had testing schemes. Of the local authorities who engaged with a testing structure, 75 per cent employed blanket testing for reading and maths across all primary schools and published the results throughout the LEA. Although the Assessment of Performance Unit did not introduce the assessment of individual teachers' performances, it did introduce the notion of testing National Curriculum subjects at certain points in a pupil's education as a basis for the national monitoring of schools.

During the 1980s, there was a plethora of educational policy documents, including 13 Education Acts and five reports confirming the government's intention to take firmer control of education. The Conservative government's focus returned to the social and academic divisiveness of schools (Lawton, 1994; Gibson and Asthana, 1999), the introduction of competitive market forces through assessment processes (Tomlinson, 2005; Chitty, 2009) and the increased pressure on teachers to raise standards of education (Lawton, 1994) through an increasing accountability and testing agenda. In 1988 a report by the Task Group on Assessment and Testing (TGAT) promoted formative and diagnostic assessment as well as summative, criterion-referenced assessment. Assessment was supposed to be positive and cumulative, an aid for teachers to plot the progress of pupils in their class. But it also provided comparative data about teachers, schools and local authorities as an explicit focus for market accountability. There was a belief that a national testing regime, appraisal and comparison of schools would lead to increased standards of education: it was a market model of education.

The Education Reform Act (DES, 1988) proposed 'radical educational measures' (Chitty, 2009: 51), the Conservative government seemingly 'gripped by a frenzied need to legislate on every aspect of education'. Power was removed from the LEAs and schools, and was handed to the Secretary of State for Education, and the government introduced the first statutory English National Curriculum (DES, 1988) for primary and secondary pupils (Lawton, 1994). It was a content-driven, assessment-focused curriculum based on pupils learning facts rather than skills (White, 2008). The Education Reform Act (DES, 1988) heralded a future education system focusing on a system of schooling subject to market forces and greater control of central government (Chitty, 2009) through an increased testing and culpability regime.

The early 1990s highlighted a Conservative government resolved to raise educational standards through a return to didactic teaching methods (Ward and Eden, 2009) and the production of an unparalleled wave of educational law-making, national testing and government regulations (Docking, 2000). In 1992, the discussion paper on *Curriculum Organisation and Classroom Practice in Primary Schools* (Alexander et al., 1992) caused much controversy. It reflected a new age of a statutory National Curriculum, Ofsted inspections and national testing (Docking, 2000). This era was typified by a government focused on control of both the economy and education in order to ensure that England prospered within the world market (Lawton, 1994). The Conservative government, during its seven years of office, was concerned with making public sector organisations like schools act in a more business-like way by creating market systems (Hatcher, 2001), and creating pressures of competition through the use of information from performance indicators such as league tables and inspections (Tomlinson, 2005). Conservative politicians were beginning to demand 'consumer-oriented education' (Hatcher, 2001). They wanted more national testing and it heralded the beginning of firm state control of education (Tomlinson, 2005; Ward and Eden, 2009), and a greater awareness of the part education plays in the economic prosperity of the country. Many education policies were issued, such as the Education Acts in 1994, 1996 and 1997, along with more accountability and a rigorous testing regime, all aimed at raising the standard of pupils' education. Since the 1944 Education Act, the government's focus has changed from being an overseer of the education system to a position where it employs overwhelming control (Bates et al., 2011). During their years in office, from 1970 to 1997, the Conservative government increased the accountability of schools through inspection and testing. By 1996 there were five parallel systems of testing in England: standardised tests for diagnostic and selection purposes operated by local authorities; the national Statutory Assessment Tests at 7, 11, 14 and 16 years of age; the GCSE and GCE bodies; vocational and occupational testing; and the informal day-to-day testing of pupils by their teachers.

As 'New' Labour took over governance of the country in 1997, the development of a world-class education system was at the top of the political agenda (Tomlinson, 2005). The New Labour government led by Blair proved to be very different from any previous Labour government with its belief in market forces and the emergence of large-scale world systems (Giddens, 1996). Government policy was a political and economic shift from the Keynesian national welfare state of former Labour governments to a state that promoted economic comparativeness in educational standards (Jessop, 2002). There was 'no shortage' of education policies – 47 education-related policies, initiatives and funding decisions were announced in just over 12 months, most of which were specifically focused on raising educational standards (Ball, 2008). The White Paper *Excellence for All Pupils* (DfEE, 1997) announced that standards would matter more than structures and there would be zero tolerance of underperformance (Docking, 2000; Tomlinson, 2005; Ball, 2008; Chitty, 2009). Schools were encouraged to set by ability, administer baseline assessments on entry to primary school, and publish literacy and numeracy standards in national performance tables (Chitty, 2009). A wealth of initiatives was introduced in an effort to raise standards, such as Educational Action Zones, and the Moser Report (1999) indicated that there were at least seven million adults in England who did not have the reading or writing skills to adequately perform daily functional tasks, such as finding a telephone number in a directory. Responding to this, the New Labour government introduced the National Curriculum 2000 (DfEE, 1999), Ofsted inspections, a greater emphasis on testing and the publication of league tables. Government policy since the 1970s has generated a series of increasingly powerful national bodies for the control of both the curriculum and assessment, including the comprehensive testing of nationally agreed level descriptors (Dearing, 1994). The results of English school pupils were now compared both nationally and internationally.

National testing

The Education Reform Act (DES, 1988) stated that there should be some way in which the education service could be assessed. The government's intentions were set out clearly in the National Curriculum document (1988). Attainment targets would be set for English, maths and science, establishing what pupils aged 7, 11, 14 and 16 should be expected to know which could be used to indicate what a pupil has learnt and to allow teachers and parents to measure pupil progress. There would be attainment targets too for other foundation subjects except for art, music and physical education (PE) where there would be guidelines only. The consultation document also indicated that there would be nationally prescribed tests taken by all pupils, administered by teachers but assessed and marked externally. The Task Group on Assessment and Testing (TGAT) was convened to consider the most appropriate forms of testing and how these could be developed for pupils of all ages throughout England. Nationally, Key Stage Statutory Assessment Tests (SATs) were introduced in the 1988 Education Reform Act and became operational in primary schools in Key Stage 1 in 1991 and Key Stage 2 in 1995. The first tests in Key Stage 1 reflected classroom practice in that activities were set for teachers to observe. Assessment Record booklets were provided for all Year 2 teachers who were required to provide evidence against all National Curriculum statements of attainment. Points were allocated depending on pupils' achievements which then translated into a National Curriculum level of attainment. But the SATs were not without their problems. For example, pupils who had watched their peers complete an activity earlier in the week were more likely to achieve high grades. Similarly, some teachers gave pupils the benefit of the doubt whilst others followed strictly the guidelines for assessment. Tasks were also time-consuming and costly. The teacher was required to work with individual pupils or small groups, meaning that another teacher needed to be employed to teach the rest of the class (Shorrocks-Taylor, 1999). By the time pupils at the end of Key Stage 2 were being assessed, Key Stage 1 pupils were already being subjected to more formalised assessments. Tests focused purely on English and maths at Key Stage 1, with science also being assessed at Key Stage 2. The focus was on factual knowledge; scientific enquiry, speaking and listening and the application of maths were not tested at this time. Key Stage 1 teachers administered the untimed tests throughout a given timescale, marked them and completed an optical mark reader sheet which was sent to the local authority for collation. Key Stage 2 teachers administered timed tests on a given date and sent pupils' work to trained external markers. Schools were then provided with the marked scripts, the National Curriculum level awarded to each pupil and the collated results of the school.

The main reason for using national tests is bound up with the information produced. Justification of such tests is that they are objective rather than subjective and so free from the biases of educators. They seek to compare pupil potential with pupil achievement and the results of these tests are placed in league tables and used by parents, local authorities and central government to measure the effectiveness of schools. As teachers, you are therefore accountable for the achievement of externally set targets at an externally set level which are then publicised externally (Dale, 1981).

International testing

The use of tests for international comparison began in 1962 with a survey of mathematics, extended later to include six further subjects. A further survey in 1980, known as the second international mathematics and science survey (SIMSS), tested maths, science, composition and classroom environment and was followed by the third survey (TIMSS) in the early 1990s. The surveys were based on sampling and on testing frameworks agreed internationally. Governments, in their pursuit of excellence, increasingly turn to international, comparative data (Zajda and Rust, 2009), evident in policy documents such as *The Importance of Teaching* (DfE, 2010b) which states that the most important measure of success is how the UK is doing compared with its international competitors.

Internationally since the early 1960s, pupils have been tested in English and maths and their results compared with the top quartile of economically advanced countries of the world which are those countries that produce two-thirds of the world's goods and services. The Programme for International Student Assessment (PISA) (OECD, 2000, 2006, 2009) is a worldwide study by the Organisation for Economic Cooperation and Development of school pupils' scholastic performance in maths, science and reading. Developed in 1997, it was first utilised in 2000 and is now repeated every three years. A single PISA cycle from start to finish takes over four years, with the results of each period of assessment taking about 18 months to be analysed. Pupils are aged between 15 years and 3 months and 16 years and 2 months at the beginning of the assessment period. Each student takes a two-hour handwritten test; part of the test is multiple-choice and part involves fuller answers. In total there are six and a half hours of assessment material, but each student is not tested on all the parts. Following the cognitive test, participating students spend a further hour answering a questionnaire on their background including learning habits, motivation and family. School directors also complete a questionnaire describing the school context such as demographics and funding. The purpose of PISA testing is to improve educational policies and outcomes, and the data has increasingly been used to assess the impact of educational quality on incomes and growth, understanding what causes differences in achievement across nations and which educational systems are offering students the best training for entering the workforce of tomorrow, and why this is so. In 2009, 470,000 15-year-old students representing 65 nations and territories participated, and, in 2012, an additional 50,000 students representing 90 nations were tested.

The Progress in International Reading Literacy Study (PIRLS) (Twist et al., 2001/2007) measures trends in pupils' reading literacy achievement and collects information about reading and literacy policies and teaching practices every five years. PIRLS (Twist et al., 2001/2007) is an important indication of the success of the government in raising standards of reading. It provides comparisons with many other countries, in terms of the attainment of pupils and strategies used to teach reading. It is an international survey which compares the reading attainment and attitudes to reading of over 200,000 10-year-old pupils around the world. It is the only international study to provide information on the reading habits of primary-aged pupils: the survey collects information not just on reading attainment, but also on pupils' reading attitudes and habits, what they read and whether they read for pleasure. Background information is also collected from head teachers and teachers and this provides further comparative information about schools and the teaching of reading. PIRLS (Twist et al., 2001) involved pupils in 49 countries around the world. Two UK nations participated in PIRLS (Twist et al., 2001); in England, 129 primary schools participated and in Northern Ireland, 136 primary schools were involved. England's performance in PIRLS (Twist et al., 2001/2007) was well above the international average and significantly higher than that attained in 2006. There was a wide range of achievement in England: the best readers were amongst the best in the world but there was a greater proportion of weaker readers than in many other high-achieving countries. The difference between the reading achievements of boys and girls was greater than that seen in many other countries. Pupils' attitudes to reading were less positive in England than the average internationally.

Michael Gove, Secretary of State for Education in 2009, claimed that the country was falling behind the rest of the world in science, literacy and maths (Bates et al., 2011) and insisted that a plan to transform England's schools was urgently needed to improve the chances of the poorest pupils. He referred to the PISA reports (OECD, 2009) which indicated that the standards of English students were falling in comparison with the other developed countries of the world.

There seems to be a belief that because national and international tests gather quantitative data then there is an objectivity which renders them accurate and meaningful. But since most of the skills measured in such tests are multidimensional, it seems illogical to force tests into a uni-dimensional structure (Goldstein and Lewis, 1996). The dilemma faced is that there are ever greater demands for national and international testing for comparative purposes whilst an increased understanding of metacognition promotes the need to measure and compare higher-order skills, which proves much more difficult. The basis of the tests at national and international level presupposes that the learner is a passive absorber of facts provided by the teacher. These tests concentrate on pupils' abilities to recall and apply facts. Even questions that are designed to test higher-order skills often merely require the recall of a formula. Pupils can succeed in these tests without a true understanding of what is being learned: this is shallow learning. Alternatively, deep learning requires the learner to control, reflect on and be committed to what and how they are learning through engagement in knowledge construction.

Assessment in the twenty-first century

Both the above national and international tests measure the attainment of one or more of the core subjects of English, maths or science but the Primary National Curriculum for England and Wales (DfE, 2014) includes many more subjects, referred to as Foundation Subjects. The proposed revised Primary Curriculum, to be taught, at the time of writing, from September 2014, similarly focuses on English, maths and science, with technology, history, geography, art, music, PE, personal, social and health education (PSHE) and modern foreign languages (the latter in Key Stage 2 only) seemingly being given less importance. Whereas there will be increased rigour in the three core subjects, the content of the other 11 subjects will be shorter in order that schools can adapt the content to the needs of their school and the local area.

However, only English and maths are tested nationally and internationally, implying that these are the most important subjects to ensure the country is economically sound and can compete with top performing countries like Finland, China and South Korea. It seems as though pupils who excel in subjects such as design technology, art and PE are less important.

Beyond the statutory assessments, teachers assess pupils' learning in all aspects of the curriculum although there are no guidelines on how this should take place. It is largely left to the teacher and the school's beliefs and values and therefore there is no consistency in this across schools or perhaps within one school. For example, pupils may be assessed on how well they work independently; the organisation and structure of their work; or their knowledge and understanding of facts. Assessment falls into two distinct sets. First, there is the behaviourist view of assessing what the learner knows, understands or can do; this is a factual base. Second, a constructivist approach, which is exploratory and investigative, assesses whether the pupil knows how and why things are the way they are (Torrance and Pryor, 1998).

National assessments of the curriculum are usually measured against predetermined criteria (criterion assessment), the pupil's previous performance (ipsative) or against other pupils (norm-referencing). National Curriculum assessments provide criterion referencing through assessing pupils against the Statements of Attainment. But many critiques of criterion referencing highlight the technical difficulties of defining the standards unambiguously and the problem of designing a qualification system that is both rigorous and flexible (Wolf, 1994).

Impact of testing

Baseline assessment, developed from the 1997 Education Act, begins as the pupil begins schooling at 4–5 years old; Reading from Six, initiated in September 2012, measures pupils' ability to read 20 genuine and 20 nonsense words by the age of 6; and the Statutory Assessment Tests are taken when the pupil is 7 years old. This means that there are national statutory tests in pupils' first three years of schooling. Although these results are not reported nationally, they are published in governors' reports, Ofsted inspections and to parents. End of Key Stage 2 SATs, administered as the pupil reaches age 11, are reported nationally in league tables.

By 1988 there were several reviews of the impact of testing on teaching and learning and pupil motivation. All suggested that tests, particularly if the results are reported, will influence both teachers and pupils as both strive for the very best results possible. But one result of this is that teachers can become too controlled in terms of what they teach and therefore lose their ability to teach other untested topics. Measurement-driven teaching influences the content of lessons so that educators purely prepare pupils for tests (Popham, 1987). The original intention of league tables was to rank schools by the results of pupils aged 7, 11 and 14. As a result of the teacher boycott of the administration of the tests, the league table ranking now rests solely with pupils aged 11. But with the publication of Key Stage 2 test results in league tables, there are high stakes for the pupil, the teacher and the school. Encouraging the comparison of schools on the basis of the performance of a set of pupils on a certain day in English and maths in their final year of primary school downgrades all other subjects in the curriculum. Moreover, league tables enable the public, parents, the local authority and the government to draw opinions about the quality of the educational provision within each school and to make comparisons between schools. Research suggests that most schools attain predictable results from the profile of their intake; a few exceed expectations and a similar number fail to attain the expected levels (Goldstein and Lewis, 1996). Typically, a school set within an area of social deprivation where there is limited parental support may attain results below age-related expectations of pupils aged 11; the results may represent outstanding achievement for that school but this is not reflected in the league tables. To some extent, this begs the question of the validity of league tables as results may be misleading. Moreover, the suitability of the Key Stage 2 SATs is questionable because all pupils in the summer term of their final year at primary school sit these tests. There is no consideration of pupils' social background, ethnicity, first language spoken or special educational need; the same test is taken whether you are a recent immigrant with limited English, a pupil from a socially deprived area or a white British pupil from a leafy suburb school, having had much parental support.

Primary schools experienced an upsurge in the data collection required from 1997 but as local authorities collated this data they were able to give schools an analysis of their performance compared with like schools such as those with a similar number of pupils entitled to free school meals. Additionally, the ability to record the percentage of pupils absent, with special educational needs or dis-applied from the tests gives some background context to the test results. Nevertheless, the tests still record the attainment not the achievement of pupils and therefore can deeply affect children's self-esteem and self-efficacy.

The way in which different pupils respond to tests depends largely on their personality, academic ability, past educational experience, current attitude, motivational state and self-efficacy. The reasons pupils provide for their success or failure are their own perceptions of their ability to succeed. Research (Linnenbrink and Pintrich, 2003) suggests that pupils with high self-efficacy engage with deep learning and can persist to overcome a problem more than other pupils. National and international tests provide competition between pupils (norm referencing) which can have a detrimental effect on pupils with low self-esteem and self-efficacy, leading to a masking of misunderstandings and a segregation of pupils into ability groupings. Within the context of the school, a minimum level of self-esteem is necessary for any learning to take place and this can be increased significantly with academic achievement (Guerney, 1987). Pupils who have positive self-esteem usually aim higher, try harder and persist in the face of difficult or challenging tasks, whereas pupils who have limited belief in themselves or their ability tend to give up when activities become difficult. Most pupils regard assessment as a summary of their success rather than indicating how they may improve, and, as a result, pupils' self-esteem can be enhanced or damaged by assessment processes. In questioning the validity and trustworthiness of national and international tests, it is debatable what purpose such tests have except for outside bodies such as Ofsted and central government.

Test results depend on both reliability and validity and the two are not entirely independent of each other. For national and international tests, reliability will be an essential prerequisite to validity; the tests would be constructed and carried out and then there need to be trained markers to reliably grade the papers. Narrowing the range of the tests enhances reliability at the expense of validity, whilst extending the tests has the opposite effect.

It is debatable whether the information gathered from national testing is valid because it seeks to compare many different cohorts. For example, it compares pupils aged 10 and 11 in different schools across England, from the leafy suburbs to the inner cities, and it compares Year 6 classes from one year to the next with different cohorts of pupils. Additionally, there is no account taken of pupils with English as an additional language, newly arrived immigrants or pupils transferring schools just before testing times. Similarly, in the national tests at Key Stage 1 there is no restriction on what can be said or on the use of another adult normally present in the classroom. There is no standardised introduction or explanation for the tasks to be executed by pupils. There is also choice in whether the teacher works one-on-one or with a small group and which personalities may constitute that group. In an attempt to ensure validity, reliability is often compromised. For example, the reading assessment for Year 2 was to select one of 20 books on the list, read aloud, then answer questions on the book, posed by the teacher. This is a valid test as it matched what would be expected of a 7-year-old pupil. However, the validity is the cause of unreliability in that there was a choice of books and often the book selected would be familiar to the pupil. Therefore, some pupils had previously read the book and so found the task easier than those who had not. Similarly, the teacher makes informal observations of the pupil based on the statement of attainment for reading at Key Stage 1, which enhances the validity of the test, but the test may not be of comparable difficulty for all pupils and there is no assurance that teachers in different schools assess their pupils to the same level in the same way. Therefore, although the reading task is more valid and less reliable, a standardised reading test would be more reliable and less valid. If national and international tests are used to measure the effectiveness of schools and for comparisons between schools, comparability of results must be robust.

International data such as the PISA (OECD, 2009) and PIRLS (Twist et al., 2007) statistics do not make allowance for the relative difficulties in learning to read in different languages. For example, English takes about twice as long to learn as a more regular language such as Finnish (Shaw, 2009). Additionally, it is generally accepted that the English language has an irregular orthography and is notorious for its irregularities and its idiosyncrasies (Sterling and Robson, 1992), resulting in a high frequency of literacy disability evident in English-speaking countries (Scott, 2004). Nor does it account for pupils tested in a language other than their native tongue or for the number of transient or immigrant pupils newly arrived in school. However, the raw data is reported in the media with comments such as: 'British school children are now ranked 23rd in the world' (Young, 2010), and used by governments as a measure of how well English schools are performing in the world rankings (The Children's Plan, DCSF, 2007).

Most teachers are concerned with the validity of the tests: will the test result be a true representation of what each pupil can do? Most politicians are more concerned with reliability: are the test results consistent and will they allow me to compare schools? Raising the stake of national and international tests through league tables and media reports that England is falling in the world rankings, enhances the ethical dimension in testing. It seems as though the higher the stake of the test result, the greater the impact on teaching, which could result in an increased prospect of cheating and unethical practice (Gipps, 1994). Clarity and equity of preparation for the tests needs addressing and teachers should be able to prepare pupils for the test they are to take, and assessment criteria should be made available to teachers and pupils and a range of assessment tasks should be included in the test in order to ensure content validity.

Accountability and testing

Accountability can be traced back as far as the 1830s when public money was used to create national schools. By 1862 inspectors were using a revised code of six standards to judge the performance of schools. More recently, schools are accountable to the public who fund them and one way in which this emerges is in the test results the school achieves each year. Assessment and testing are the gatekeepers on the boundary between the internal work of schools and the public interest in controlling that work (Black, 1998). Accountability has moral, financial and legal elements (Headington, 2003). Teachers are morally and legally bound to provide an appropriate education for all pupils and to report regularly on the progress of pupils to a variety of stakeholders. The head teacher and governing body have a legal responsibility to administer the public funding effectively for the benefit of all pupils. The school has a responsibility to the local authority and to the Department for Education. There has long been accountability connected to the education system with the school self-evaluation document, Ofsted and HMI reports, publicising exam results and the national and local monitoring of standards.

As a teacher, you are primarily accountable to your pupils, responsible for providing lessons which are stimulating, challenging and interesting, ensuring that pupils progress through continuous evaluation and assessment. You are also accountable to the parents of pupils for their educational development and are required to report to parents the test results that indicate the progress made, at certain intervals throughout the year. Teachers are also accountable to their colleagues by providing accurate data so that pupils' progress can be tracked, to share good practice and to support the development of the profession. Finally, teachers are responsible to the taxpayer as they are funded by the government. This is illustrated through Ofsted reports, SATs, performance tables and other reports such as those supplied by the media.

The coalition Conservative/Liberal Democrat government elected in May 2010 prepared the education system for a further radical change in education policy. *The Importance of Teaching* (DfE, 2010b) declared that action was needed to raise standards by holding schools to account for the results they achieve. A rise in standards, the document (2010b) pro-claimed, would be attained through national testing and league tables. Standards, or the expected level of attainment, have been referred to frequently for well over 100 years. For example, level 2b is expected of pupils at the end of Year 2 whilst level 4 is expected of pupils aged 11. Standards do not change but performance does; new standards are set as there are developments in overall improvement (Pring, 1996).

Since 1990, there has been an ever greater involvement of central government in schools in the drive to raise standards, using an increasing collection of accountability and testing systems. During the years 1979 to 2007, initiatives and interventions were laid over each other (Butt and Gunter, 2007b), but, at the same time, the government proposed to re-focus Ofsted inspections and strengthen the performance measures used to hold schools accountable through a rigorous testing regime.

However, whether increased testing improves learning is debata-ble. It encourages superficial learning, teaching to tests and a narrow curriculum focused on the core subjects of English, maths and sci-ence. Indeed, the promotion of testing as an important component of establishing a competitive market in education can be very harmful (Black et al., 2002). Greater accountability through increased testing is flawed because of the regional and local differences in school population and even economists admit that the current testing sys-tems are not strong predictors of economic success. Nevertheless, standards of education seem to have become surrogate for the strength of the economy (Rizvi and Lingard, 2010) – a 'steering from a distance' policy (Kickert, 1991).

The focus on raising educational standards in England through a testing culture implies that global events affect the English school sys-tem (Spring, 2009). One of the key issues is the poor levels of schools' achievements indicated in national and international tests, which is used as evidence to threaten economic prosperity (Ball et al., 2007). For example, the Leitch Report (2006) strongly implies that without an increase in educational standards, the country will condemn itself to a lingering decline in competitiveness, diminishing economic growth and a bleaker future for all its citizens. In effect, globalisation and standards of education are inextricably linked, but this places a raised pressure on schools to evidence increased standards of education through national and international testing.

There are three inevitable effects of the accountability and testing agenda: schools will be unwilling to take on pupils with learning difficulties, since they affect test results; teachers will concentrate their efforts on pupils who are borderline between one level and the next to boost results; and practising for the tests will limit the curriculum taught (Ball, 2008).

A more analytical rather than hierarchical assessment system would measure pupil achievement rather than attainment and be formative rather than summative in nature. Similarly, the reporting of attainment is flawed in that it uses a single overall figure as a test result rather than dealing with the complexity of the different domains being assessed. The historical approach requires data that can be added up to create averages, modes and means (Gipps, 1994) but the reliability of educational assessment requires consideration of pupil profiles across and within subjects, reporting qualitative descriptions of achievement that are formative in nature.

The form of the test has little impact on teachers or teaching; it is the political and economic use made of the scores that determines the effect of tests (Smith, 1991). Similarly, the coalition government of 2010 requires the attainment rather than the achievement of pupils to be reported. Previously, value-added achievements were collated that measured the progress of pupils from their starting point at age 4 up to the age of 11. Removing the value-added perspective leaves the norm-referenced approach that measures what each pupil has attained, taking no consideration of their starting point. This means that pupils who enter school at age 4 with limited spoken or written language are expected to achieve level 4 at age 11, as well as those pupils who enter schooling already reading and writing.

Assessment in the form of written tests began in the 19th century and came out of the need for increased social justice in a developing society which required more trained professionals and a more literate workforce (McLeod, 1982). Examinations were seen as a way to raise standards and were the means by which recruitment to a profession was judged.

Few people would dispute that it is essential that teachers strive to ensure that all pupils reach their potential, and that schools and staff should prepare pupils for lifelong learning and the obligations of citizenship (Morrow and Torres, 2000), but schools operate under government legislation, regulations, financial constraints and, increasingly, a testing and accountability culture. Generally, central government does not invite public opinion (Elmore, 1989), or teacher opinion, when developing educational law; rather, such laws are driven by developments in society and increasingly by England's position in world OECD rankings (Elmore, 1989).

Continuous reform of the structure and culture of the English education system has taken place since the Second World War (Bates et al.,

2011) through a programme of accountability such as league tables, Ofsted inspections, national and international testing. The onus placed on schools to provide data about standardised testing and the requirement to publish test results underline the importance of the national testing structure, and yet such results are often interpreted uncritically and out of context. They are used to satisfy bureaucratic criteria rather than being professionally analysed by teachers, which could draw out the true meaning of them (Gipps and Goldstein, 1983).

To conclude, education is now regarded as our best economic policy. Unfortunately, whenever there is a focus on accountability and performativity, it seems as though only the core subjects are of value. Increasing the capacity of pupils is the ultimate goal in education and assessment is a vital part of this. Achieving lifelong learning can only be achieved if pupils self-assess and own their learning so that they can monitor and improve their knowledge and understanding of the curriculum both inside and outside school. Improved learning requires thoughtful, reflective and interactive discussion and formative assessment between pupil and teacher. The next chapter explores the principles of assessment.

Points for Reflection

- What is the purpose of assessment and testing?
- Does testing improve learning?
- Are testing, standards and accountability interlinked?
- How important is the pupil in the accountability and testing culture of the twenty-first century?

Further Reading

Ball, S. (2008) *The Education Debate*. Bristol: The Policy Press.

Dale, R. (1981) *From Expectations to Outcomes in Educational Systems*. Milton Keynes: Open University Press.

Gillard, D. (2011) *Education in England: A Brief History*. Available at: www.educationengland.org.uk (accessed 10/02/11).

Gunter, H. (2007) 'Remodelling the School Workforce in England: A Study in Tyranny', *Journal for Critical Education Policy Studies*, 5(1): 1–15.

Hatcher, R. (2001) 'Getting Down to Business: Schooling in the Globalised Economy', *Education and Social Justice*, 3(2): 45–59.

CHAPTER 3

ASSESSING THE PROGRESS OF PUPILS IN THE EARLY YEARS

Chapter Objectives

1 To understand the importance of monitoring young pupils' work
2 To understand the statutory assessments required for young pupils
3 To understand the role of parents in the assessment of young pupils

All pupils' progress must be monitored in order that teaching can be adjusted to constantly challenge and extend pupils' learning. This includes the youngest of pupils in nursery and early years settings. However, it is evident that they are unable to perform written tests and, with very young pupils, speech may also be too underdeveloped to make valid assessments. This chapter first examines the requirement of the Early Years Foundation Stage (EYFS) curriculum and explores the assessment of progress in very young pupils using the Early Years Foundation Stage Profile (EYFSP). It then considers the national tests that early years pupils are required to complete and the role of parents in the assessment of these young pupils. Finally, there will be a range of assessment types and formats that practitioners may find useful in the assessment of early years pupils.

Early Years Foundation Stage

Modern ideals of early childhood education emerged from practices developed in Germany in the early 18th century (Wright, 2010). Most young children under the age of 5 are looked after by at least one parent or carer and this has always been so, but prior to the Second World War most young children were cared for by servants, nannies, grandparents or neighbours. Although data from this time is scarce, research by the Equality and Human Rights Commission (King 2010) indicates that many grandparents helped their children into employment by caring for grandchildren, sometimes retiring from paid work themselves to do so. Today, an estimated one third of working mothers rely on grandparents for childcare, and one in four of all working families of very young children, (43 per cent), with mothers who are employed, are looked after by grandparents. Although there are no long-term reliable statistics, data suggests that despite working-class grandparents usually taking a role in nurturing their very young grandchild(ren), this is a relatively new thing amongst the middle classes, where more mothers of young children are now likely to be in paid work than in the past (Wright, 2010).

Care and education of young children and their mothers was evident in the late 18th century, with trained volunteers visiting families to offer advice on infant care, diet and cleanliness in some local authorities. There was little government action on the education of young children, until the First World War, when the government funded day nurseries for pupils under 3 and nursery schools for pupils aged 3–5, because women were needed in the workforce to regenerate the economy after the devastation of the war (Thane, 2011).

After the Second World War, the state increasingly took responsibility for early childhood education and by the 1950s and 1960s it was most common for mothers to take time out from work to care for their children whilst they were young. Since 1966 governments have provided a more formal framework for early childhood education. In 1966, the DfEE produced *Desirable Outcomes for Children's Learning on Entering Compulsory Education*, aimed at assessing the standards of pupils aged 5. There were several areas that had to be assessed:

- Personal and social development, including play and relationships
- Language and literacy

- Mathematics
- Knowledge and understanding of the world
- Physical development
- Creative development.

Over 30 years later in 1997, the White Paper *Excellence for All Pupils* identified that the government recognised that children benefit from early years education and they laid down plans for its development in England through early years development of partnerships and plans. The long-term aim was to develop a comprehensive and integrated approach to the education of young children, with different providers working in partnership to enhance learning opportunities for young children. In September 1998, it became necessary for the early years development partnerships to ensure a free part-time education place for all 4-year-olds whose parents wanted it. In 1999 Sure Start was introduced. Sure Start Children's Centres provide an integrated service for young children and their families. They align early education, childcare, health and family support. Services provided include advice on health care and child development, play schemes, parenting classes, family outreach support and adult education and advice. Children's centres play a crucial role in early intervention, ensuring families who need them the most can access help and support when needed. By 2000, the Early Years Foundation Stage (DfEE, 2000) had been introduced for pupils aged 3–5 and in 2004 the government ensured free pre-school education for all 3-year-olds. There is now an approved Early Years Development and Childcare Plan for every local authority which is recognition of the fact that it is essential for early years pupils to have access to good quality education. By 2012 there was a *Statutory Framework for the Early Years Foundation Stage* (DfE, 2012) which covers the learning expected of children from birth to age 5. It has four principles:

- Every child is a competent learner from birth who can be resilient, capable, confident and self-assured; each child is unique.
- Children learn to be strong and independent from a base of a loving and caring relationship with parents/carers.
- The environment plays a key role in supporting and extending children's development and learning.
- Children develop and learn in different ways and at different rates and all areas of learning and development are equally important and interconnected.

This document sets the standard that all early years providers must meet to ensure that children learn and develop well and are kept healthy and safe. It gives children a broad range of knowledge and skills for good future progress through school and life and takes account of the fact that every child is unique and learns and develops in their own way and at their own pace. There are seven areas of learning, three of which are seen as vital for promoting curiosity, generating an enthusiasm for learning and building relationships:

- Communication and language
- Physical activity
- Personal, social and emotional learning

The other four are:

- Literacy
- Mathematics
- Understanding the world
- Expressive arts and design.

As can be seen above, these areas are very similar to those published in 1966 in *Desirable Outcomes for Children's Learning on Entering Compulsory Education* (DfEE, 1966).

Assessment of the seven areas of learning above is vital in order to ascertain the level at which pupils are working and plan future activities which challenge and extend their learning. Within the *Statutory Framework for the Early Years Foundation Stage* (DfE, 2012), the Early Learning Goals are set out and there are clear guidelines for the EYFS Profile which is the assessment tool.

Last century, the culture of early childhood testing was based on assumptions of a genetic base of individual differences between children (Wright, 2010). Jean Piaget was a Swiss developmental psychologist and philosopher known for his epistemological studies with children. His views of how children's minds work and develop have been enormously influential in educational theory, his particular insight being children's increasing capacity to understand the world in which they live. He suggested that they cannot undertake certain tasks until they are psychologically mature enough to do so. He also proposed that children's thinking does not develop on a smooth and predictable pathway but that there are certain points at which it 'takes off'. Although he never intended for the four phases of development to be age-bound, he identified the 'take-off' points happening at about 18 months, 7 years and 11 or 12 years, it has been taken to mean that before these ages children are not capable (no matter how bright) of understanding things in certain ways, and has been used as the basis for scheduling the school curriculum. Much of the criticism of Piaget's work (1936) centred on his research methods, as much of his work was based on observations of his three well-educated children.

Other scholars, such as Vygotsky (1978) and Bruner (1957), challenged Piaget's (1936) thinking in that they believed that learning and development are social operations and that interaction with the environment, peers and adults can affect the ways and speed at which pupils develop. Moreover, most children possess skills at an earlier age and are much less egocentric at age 4 or 5 than Piaget (1936) predicted. Nevertheless, few people would disagree that the work of Piaget has had an impact on early years curricula and assessment in the twenty-first century.

Assessment gained from a range of sources is an integral part of pupils' education and aids decision making in ensuring appropriate learning and/or an intervention strategy. It does not aim to capture the whole pupil's personality and achievements but it does provide information on the pupil's typical performance in certain areas (Sainsbury, 2004). In order to further pupils' learning, it is important to know how they respond in different situations, what kinds of things interest them, in what areas they are most confident, what areas seem challenging and what can be done to further their learning and development (Hutchin, 2012). From the early days of a child's life, parents, carers, nursery teachers, childminders and early years practitioners need to be aware of a child's normal development and growth patterns (Mindes, 2011). The EYFSP requires assessment of pupils aged between 2 and 3. There is no requirement for this to entail excessive paperwork (Tickell, 2011) but early years practitioners need to inform parents and carers of their child's progress through a short written report that highlights the child's strengths and areas of concern. If there are significant emerging concerns, or an identified special educational need or disability, practitioners should develop a targeted plan to support the child's future learning and development involving other professionals such as the provider's Special Educational Needs Coordinator (SENCo) (DfE, 2012).

In the final term in which pupils reach the age of 5, the EYFS Profile must be completed. This is an assessment of pupils' knowledge, understanding and skills within the Early Learning Goals and their readiness to enter Year 1 with the demands of the National Curriculum. When the EYFSP was introduced in 2003, it was seen to be innovative in that it had no set tasks or tests and it involved parents and carers in its judgements.

The revised EYFSP (2012) is less bureaucratic although it retains the inventiveness of the original document (Hutchin, 2012). It adheres to the following principles:

- It has a clear purpose and outcome.
- It is focused on exactly the information needed.
- It evidences what the pupil *can* do.
- It begins with the pupil not a set of predetermined tasks.
- The assessments are an integral part of the early years practitioner's daily tasks.
- Data are used to determine the pupil's next steps in learning.
- Consideration is given to *how* the pupil learns.
- Parents/carers and pupils are involved in the assessment process.
- Records of achievement are regularly reviewed and shared with parents/carers. (Drummond, 1999; Hutchin, 2012)

In summary, assessments are systematic, multidisciplinary and based on everyday tasks completed by pupils. They should be comprehensive in that they gather data about all developmental areas (Mindes, 2011).

The Early Years Foundation Stage (EYFS) is the statutory framework published in 2012 by the Department for Education that sets the standards for the development, learning and care of children from birth to age 5 (DfE, 2012). It summarises pupils' attainment at age 5 and is based on continual daily observations in which the pupil demonstrates achievements in all seven areas of the EYFS (DfE, 2012) independently, consistently and in a range of contexts. The final judgement is made in consultation with parents or carers and other professionals involved in pupils' learning.

A completed EYFS Profile consists of 20 points of information relating to the 17 Early Learning Goals descriptors and a short narrative describing pupils' learning characteristics. Early years practitioners should decide whether each child has met the expected level of attainment, exceeded or failed to attain it and record it accordingly as: *expected, exceeding* or *emerging*. Once information has been gathered from each school, it is internally and externally moderated before the data is sent to the local authority and the DfE.

Early Learning Goals

ELG 01 Listening and attention: Children listen attentively in a range of situations. They listen to stories, accurately anticipating key events, and respond to what they hear with relevant comments, questions or actions. They give their attention to what others say and respond appropriately, whilst engaged in another activity.

ELG 02 Understanding: Children follow instructions involving several ideas or actions. They answer 'how' and 'why' questions about their experiences and in response to stories or events.

ELG 03 Speaking: Children express themselves effectively, showing awareness of listeners' needs. They use past, present and future forms accurately when talking about events that have happened or are to happen in the future. They develop their own narratives and explanations by connecting ideas or events.

ELG 04 Moving and handling: Children show good control and coordination in large and small movements. They move confidently in a range of ways, safely negotiating space. They handle equipment and tools effectively, including a pencil for writing.

ELG 05 Health and self-care: Children know the importance for good health of physical exercise and a healthy diet, and talk about ways to keep healthy and safe. They manage their own basic hygiene and personal needs successfully, including dressing and going to the toilet independently.

ELG 06 Self-confidence and self-awareness: Children are confident to try new activities, and to say why they like some activities more than others. They are confident to speak in a familiar group, will talk about their ideas and will choose the resources they need for their chosen activities. They say when they do or don't need help.

ELG 07 Managing feelings and behaviour: Children talk about how they and others show feelings, talk about their own and others' behaviour, and its consequences, and know that some behaviour is unacceptable. They work as part of a group or class, and understand and follow rules. They adjust their behaviour to different situations, and take changes of routine in their stride.

ELG 08 Making relationships: Children play cooperatively, taking turns with others. They take account of one another's ideas about how to organise their activity. They show sensitivity to others' needs and feelings, and form positive relationships with adults and other children.

ELG 09 Reading: Children read and understand simple sentences. They use phonic knowledge to decode regular words and read them aloud accurately. They also read some common irregular words. They demonstrate an understanding when talking with others about what they have read.

ELG 10 Writing: Children use their phonic knowledge to write words in ways which match their spoken sounds. They also write some irregular common words. They write sentences which can be read by themselves and others. Some words are spelt correctly and others are phonetically plausible.

ELG 11 Numbers: Children count reliably with numbers from one to 20, place them in order and say which number is one more or one less than a given number. Using quantities and objects, they add and subtract two single-digit numbers and count on or back to find the answer. They solve problems, including doubling, halving and sharing.

ELG 12 Shape, space and measures: Children use everyday language to talk about size, weight, capacity, position, distance, time and money to compare quantities and objects and to solve problems. They recognise, create and describe patterns. They explore characteristics of everyday objects and shapes and use mathematical language to describe them.

ELG 13 People and communities: Children talk about past and present events in their own lives and in the lives of family members. They know that other children don't always enjoy the same things, and are sensitive to this. They know about similarities and differences between themselves and others, and amongst families, communities and traditions.

ELG 14 The world: Children know about similarities and differences in relation to places, objects, materials and living things. They talk about the features of their own immediate environment and how environments might vary from one to another. They make observations of animals and plants and explain why some things occur, and talk about changes.

ELG 15 Technology: Children recognise that a range of technology is used in places such as homes and schools. They select and use technology for particular purposes.

ELG 16 Exploring and using media and materials: Children sing songs, make music and dance, and experiment with ways of changing them. They safely use and explore a variety of materials, tools and techniques, experimenting with colour, design, texture, form and function.

ELG 17 Being imaginative: Children use what they have learnt about media and materials in original ways, thinking about uses and purposes. They represent their own ideas, thoughts and feelings through design and technology, art, music, dance, role play and stories.

National tests

In addition to the Early Learning Goals, pupils in the early years of schooling are subjected to two further national tests, resulting in pupils in the first three years of their schooling in England being assessed against national benchmarks. Whilst it is common knowledge that children develop more in the formative years of their life than at any other stage in their lives, national testing at ages 5, 6 and 7 could be regarded as excessive.

As seen above, the Early Learning Goals are the culmination of five years of following and being tracked through the EYFS. Pupils reach milestones from birth and practitioners record these on the EYFSP which provides an overview of the profile of each child at 5 years of age. One year later, pupils must engage with a further national test, this time to check on their knowledge, understanding and application of phonics. Reading by Six was borne out of research resulting in the publication: *Reading by Six: How the Best Schools Do It* (DfE, 2010a), which based its evidence on a sample of 12 schools which adopt a very demanding and sequential approach to developing speaking and listening and teaching reading, writing and spelling through an intensive approach to systematic synthetic phonics. It is based on government feeling that the foundations for competent reading are laid down between the ages of 3 and 7. There seems to be a fundamental misunderstanding that phonic knowledge equates to skilled reading. It is possible to decode the words in this test but be unable to read, just as an adult is able to decode and read words of an unknown foreign language but fail to understand what they mean.

Teaching unions indicate that their members agree that phonics is a good way of teaching children to read but say it is one of a range of techniques used by teachers, who should be trusted to vary their methods depending on their pupils. The check may be flawed because it cannot be used to read all words, such as 'come', 'said' and 'once', which require other techniques. On a further note, it is possible that the check will lead to teachers teaching to the test and cause anxiety for pupils (and their parents) who fail to read all 40 words of the test.

Nevertheless, the government states that the phonic check is based on a method that is internationally proven to get results and that pupils who *fail* the test will get the extra help needed to become good readers (DfE, 2010a). However, research revealed that no skilled reader uses phonics alone (Shaw, 2012) and it is therefore important to teach pupils transcoding from spelling to sound (Sterling and Robson, 1992). Many pupils use context for reading but the words in the Reading by Six test are individual and unrelated. Furthermore, as long as pupils gain the ability to read, it does not follow that this will result in a lifetime's love of reading (DfE, 2010a); not all adults enjoy reading even if they are skilled readers.

From September 2012, all children aged 6 in England were required to take the phonics screening check, in addition to Year 2 pupils who failed to meet the required standard in Year 1. The Reading by Six test involves the decoding of 40 words – 20 real words and 20 nonsense words such as *vap* and *vog* – although any two-syllable words assessed are real words because the government found difficulty in inventing polysyllabic pseudo-words. The phonics screening check is divided into two sections:

Section 1 is concerned with grapheme-phoneme correspondences that are usually introduced first to children who are learning to decode using phonics and simple word structures.

Section 2 includes grapheme-phoneme correspondences that are generally introduced to children later and that correspond to more than one phoneme plus more complex word structures, including two-syllable words.

There are four words on a page and it takes approximately five to seven minutes per child or over three hours for a class of 30 pupils, although there is no time limit and children are given enough time to respond to each word. It could be that the test confuses the brightest pupils as they try to make real words from the pseudo ones: many, for example, read the word *storm* for *strom* and fail to get that point. In fact, the pilot indicated that only 32 per cent of 6-year-olds who took the screening check reached the appropriately challenging expected level, questioning the purpose and validity of the test.

The following year, as pupils reach 7 years of age, they are required to take further tests in reading, writing, speaking and listening, maths and science. These are the Key Stage 1 Standard Attainment Tasks (SATs) which are administered and marked by the class teacher but are national tests which are reported to parents, governors, the local authority and the government. It involves you as the teacher summarising your judgements on children's attainment in relation to the National Curriculum level descriptions for each child. You need to determine the levels for reading, writing and speaking and listening, plus an overall subject level for both maths and science. Within maths, more weighting should be placed on number which includes handling data than the other areas of shape, space and measures and using and applying maths which each count for one fifth of the pupil's overall performance. Likewise in science, scientific enquiry accounts for three times as much as the other attainment targets of life processes and living things, materials and their properties and physical processes.

Schools must use the 2007 and 2009 Key Stage 1 National Curriculum tests for English and maths that they have already or they can order further copies from the National Curriculum Authority tools website. There are no test booklets for science and attainment in this subject is based on teacher assessment throughout the year. You will administer the tests to help you arrive at a secure judgement for your final teacher assessment level for pupils aged 7. As a minimum, you must administer a task or test in reading, writing and maths for each child, except those judged to be working below level 1. The tests are available at Level 1 to Level 5 for pupils in the primary school and it is your responsibility to decide at which level of the tests the pupil is working. The tasks and tests can be used at any time of the year but can only be used once and they should not be used to prepare pupils for the assessments (DfE, 2012). They must be administered under appropriate conditions to ensure all schools are administering them to agreed national standards. Results for all pupils should be reported to parents, local authorities and the DfE. For pupils who are working below level 1, a P scale must be reported. P scales are smaller measures of progress and are discussed more fully in the next chapter.

External moderation of Key Stage 1 results ensures teacher judgements are accurate and consistent nationally, and are therefore valid for school accountability as a baseline for measuring progress. Schools will receive an external moderation visit at least once every four years. This entails checking that the teacher understands the standards by examining their evidence for awarding certain levels to pupils in their class.

Therefore, in a pupil's first three years of compulsory schooling, by the time they are 7 years of age, they will have been subjected to at least three national tests – the EYFSP, the Reading by Six test and the Key Stage 1 SATs, whilst pupils in some other European countries are just beginning their compulsory school life at age 7.

Assessing, recording and reporting the progress of early years pupils

You will need to gather evidence of the progress of all pupils not only to inform your judgements in the national EYFSP and SATs but also in order to plan day-to-day lessons that are interesting and enjoyable but challenging and demanding, ensuring pupils' progress in their learning. Whereas the national tests are a summative judgement, assessment to support and extend learning is formative. Assessment to promote learning in the early years should include assessment of the pupil's care and well-being. This includes ensuring the environment is inclusive, challenging and exciting, inspiring pupils to explore and learn.

One of the ways in which early years pupils can be assessed is to listen to their ideas, discussions and explanations as they play, and engage them in conversation. Drummond (1999) explains this as *seeing* the learning. A further suggestion is self- and peer assessment, although probably the most common approach to assessment in the early years is through observations (Pidmore and Luff, 2012).

Listening to and talking with pupils provides an opportunity to discover aspects of their personality, behaviours and learning that perhaps might not be available from another source. In the twenty-first century, in a highly technological society which offers little opportunity for young children to hear good modelling of the use of language or communication, it is important to encourage the skill of conversation in very young pupils. Pupils' conversations, if encouraged, can reveal their needs and interests and, because they can learn from almost everything they do, see or touch, there is potential for assessment of the conversation or discussion that ensues. For example, by jumping in a puddle, pupils will learn not only that rain made the puddle in a hole or dip in the ground and that they will get wet feet but also that, as they jump in the puddle, the water jumps out – the basis of displacement theory. Through listening to what the pupil rationalises from this experience and engaging in conversation to extend the learning, assessment can take place.

Self- and peer assessment can be encouraged by the teacher allowing the pupil enough time to reflect on their experience or on how they did something – such as building a tower with bricks. If the tower falls down easily, how can it be made more rigid? It is important to develop self- and peer assessment in young pupils because it enables them to take control of some of their learning; it generates a sense of responsibility and self-esteem, and offers opportunities to be involved in real-life problem solving. Pupils may also take responsibility for the organisation of learning spaces, labelling resources and offering advice on how to improve their own and others' learning in plenary sessions, all of which encourage their motivation to learn. The teacher, through understanding the way in which pupils think and operate, can achieve more accurate assessments of their growing knowledge and understanding of language, relationships and the world in which they live.

Another way of recording assessment data is through learning stories. The Te Whāriki approach, initiated by Carr (2001) in New Zealand, is a sociocultural curriculum based on the theories of Vygotsky (1978) that promotes the fact that children learn what is valued and useful in their communities through shared relationships and activities with others. Although this approach is closely linked with the early years curriculum in New Zealand, it is easily adapted to the EYFS in England where there is access to a rich source of information from a variety of stakeholders. Learning is assessed by understanding what it is pupils are trying to achieve. It is about motivating and supporting pupils to improve their knowledge and understanding through learning stories (Carr, 2001). Learning stories capture children's learning in story format and combine observation and documentation. The story gives the context of the learning, the contribution of participants and the learning they demonstrate. Teachers can gain an understanding of how the children feel about themselves, others and their activities. There are four steps to a learning story: capturing the story, analysing it, deciding the next steps and implementing the improvement plans (Hutchin, 2012). Learning stories can help to review learning as teachers probe further by asking questions such as: Why did you build it that way? What do you mean when you say...? Can you think of other ways? (Carr, 2001).

Observation is perhaps the most used strategy to gather assessment data from pupils in their early years and is a key aspect of the role of the early years practitioner. Observation is the basis for many educational decisions made many times throughout the day as teachers and early years practitioners decide what to teach or what activities to set out, what resources to use and whether an activity will be adult or child led. You will learn more about the pupils in your care through observation than by any other form of assessment (Mindes, 2011). There are four types of observations:

- participant observations where the adult and pupil engage in adult-led activity
- incidental observations which are significant observations that happen without adult intervention
- samples which are pupils' markings, artwork, etc.
- conversations and interactions between adult and pupil that offer information on how the pupil thinks and communicates.

The observation process can improve the quality, care and learning opportunities offered to pupils, suggest how to improve the finer details of the programme of activities to extend pupils' learning and offer insights into the ways in which pupils operate in a variety of situations.

Observation can take place during any activity and in any context in which the pupil is engaged and involves reaching an understanding of children's learning by watching, listening and interacting as they engage in everyday activities, events and experiences, and demonstrate their specific knowledge, skills and understanding. It is the most reliable way of building up an accurate picture of children's development and learning. Observation can be planned or unplanned but should aim to gather assessment data on the seven areas of learning in the EYFS, and be on a mixture of teacher- and pupil-directed activity and the pupil working with peers and with other adults (Sainsbury, 2004).

Observational assessment does not require prolonged breaks from interaction with children, nor excessive written recording, but is likely to be interwoven into interactions or conversations either with peers or adults. Whatever is recorded should be succinct and useful. Some observations will be planned but some may spontaneously capture an important action that evidences attainment in one or more areas of learning. Some observation data will be lengthy, some will be brief notes, some written formally such as a miscue analysis of reading, and some more casually through reflection at a later date on an earlier activity or incident. Often, observation of a pupil's learning is incidental and therefore the recording of data needs to be simple yet effective, such as jottings on a Post-it note, a photograph or a video clip.

The role of parents in the assessment of young children

Historically, the education of the child rested with practitioners in the school or setting. Although, as explained above, it is still the responsibility of the early years practitioner, along with the head teacher and governors of the school or setting, to collect assessment data on the progress of the pupils in their care, gaining a full picture of the child's progress is a collaborative activity which involves parents. It could be that the child behaves very differently at home to when in the school or setting. Research, such as that by Siraj-Blatchford et al. (2004) and Ofsted (2008b), indicates that involving parents in pupils' education has a significant positive impact on their development and learning, and the revised EYFS (2012) focuses on developing this relationship, stating that parents should be equal partners with the practitioner in completing the EYFS Profile. Parents should be provided with the opportunity to report on their child's developmental level and raise any concerns or worries.

Parents may be involved in day-to-day events and daily conversations, special events such as Christmas plays, curriculum and parents' evenings, in celebrating achievements and in the learning and assessment of the pupil. There may be a settling-in phase as the pupil enters Foundation 2 from nursery, and the assessment process can begin as that transition is planned so that a full picture of the child can be ready for when they enter the main school setting. Reports from parents may cover a wide range of information, such as medical history, current development, personality, social and emotional adjustments and family background, that can affect the child's learning.

Of course, it may be that the parent or guardian is not the person to drop off the child because of work commitments or medical complications. It is therefore important to build a firm relationship with the link person so that they may liaise with parents when the pupil returns home. Home–school books, journals and learning journeys can all be shared and added to by parents/carers at different stages, starting from the initial baseline meeting as the pupil enters a new stage of their early childhood education.

It may be that the school or setting wishes to have a policy on parental involvement which can be monitored regularly for impact, but there are perhaps four key points in relation to developing a successful partnership between parents and practitioners:

- listening attentively and noting additional things such as intonation of voice and non-verbal communication, allowing the parent/carer to ask more questions than you

- providing information in clear lay person's language, offering an opportunity for the parent/carer to ask questions

- time for talk and time within the conversation for both parties to reflect and collect thoughts

- a summary of the key points throughout the conversation and at the end, which is important to ensure a shared understanding of the main points (Hutchin, 2012).

Finally, some parents may be reluctant to become involved in their child's learning and assessment for a range of reasons, such as a bad experience when they were at school, a belief that it is not their role to educate their child or worries about the perceived power divide, and it may fall to the early years practitioner to be proactive in developing a secure relationship. Making learning visible to parents, having regular conversations with them and inviting them to celebrate their child's achievements should gradually encourage them to realise the benefits of an effective relationship between home and school or setting.

Points for Reflection

- Pupils engage in three nationally reported assessments between the ages of 5 and 7.
- It is important that assessments of early years pupils are meaningful and record key milestones in their learning and development.
- Practitioners should address any learning and development needs in partnership with parents/carers and any relevant professionals.

Further Reading

Carr, M. (2001) *Assessment in Early Childhood Settings: Learning Stories*. London: SAGE.

Dunlop, A.W. and Fabian, H. (2007) *Informing Transitions in the Early Years*. Maidenhead: Open University Press.

Morrow, L. (2001) *Literacy Development in the Early Years*. London: Taylor & Francis.

Thane, P. (2011) 'The History of Early Years Child Care'. A discussion paper based on a presentation at the Department for Education, 6 October.

Wright, R.J., Martland, J. and Stafford, A.K. (2006) *Early Numeracy: Assessment for Teaching and Interventions*. London: SAGE.

Success!!

Today _____ successfully managed to

_____

_____

_____

Well done _____ !

Signed _____

Figure 3.1   Celebrating achievements in the early years

Photocopiable: *Understanding Assessment in Primary Education*
© Sue Faragher, 2014 (SAGE)

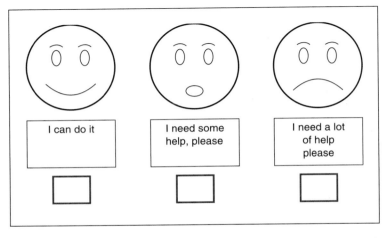

Figure 3.1.1 Early years self-assessment (alter the words for peer assessment)

 Photocopiable: *Understanding Assessment in Primary Education*
© Sue Faragher, 2014 (SAGE)

My name is _____

I am _____ years old

I go to _____ school

My teacher is _____

This is a picture of me at school

My friends are _____

Date:

Things I like to do (can include pictures):
*
*
*
Things I am good at:
*
*
*
Date:

Things I find difficult (can include pictures):
*
*
Things I want to get better at doing:
*
*
Date:

Figure 3.1.2 Early years learning journey

The pages can then be repeated at certain milestones in the pupil's early education.

 Photocopiable: *Understanding Assessment in Primary Education*
© Sue Faragher, 2014 (SAGE)

Fine Motor Skills Check	Name:		Date:
Skill	Emerging	Expected	Exceeding
Zips			
Buttons			
Strings beads			
Bead patterns			
Controls writing tools			
Uses scissors correctly			

Early Mathematics	Name:		Date:
Skill	Emerging	Expected	Exceeding
Names colours: Red Yellow Green Purple Orange …			
Names basic 2D shapes: Square Rectangle Circle Triangle …			
Recognises numbers to 5:			

Early Reading	Name:		Date:
Skill	Emerging	Expected	Exceeding
Knows print left to right			
Turns pages right to left			
Listens attentively to stories			
Follows simple instructions			
Asks why/how questions			
Speaks clearly and audibly			
Uses past, present and future tenses correctly			

Figure 3.1.3   Observational Sheet examples

The words can be replaced with whatever assessment is taking place

Photocopiable: *Understanding Assessment in Primary Education*
© Sue Faragher, 2014 (SAGE)

CHAPTER 4

ASSESSING PUPILS WITH SPECIAL EDUCATIONAL NEEDS

Chapter Objectives

1 To recognise the effect of self-esteem and self-efficacy on the achievement of pupils with SEN
2 To gain a range of strategies to assess pupils with SEN
3 To understand the purpose and use of P scales

There are many types and purposes of assessment in primary school but the method of collating it and using it to inform teaching or a relevant intervention strategy remains the same (Raynor, 2007). Assessment should provide information on the pupil's strengths and areas for development that may suggest the pupil requires support in one or more areas of the curriculum. A comparison with peers' attainment provides an indication of the level of extra support needed by the pupil with special educational needs (SEN) but does not provide conclusive evidence (Littleboy et al., 2000). In an ideal world, every pupil would have an Individual Education Plan (IEP) but this of course is not possible due to a lack of resources. For every assessment, however, particularly for those involving pupils with SEN and their increased vulnerability, assessments must have a purpose, should be valid and reliable and have some meaning for you and your colleagues, and for parents and carers (Lieberman and Houston-Wilson, 2002).

Since the Warnock Report of 1978, there have been an increasing number of pupils with SEN in primary schools who are entitled to have full access to the National Curriculum. It is estimated that there are approximately one in five, or 1.7 million, pupils with SEN in English schools (Ofsted, 2010). *Supporting Aspiration: A New Approach to Special Educational Needs and Disability* (DfE, 2011) states that a disability is something that has a long-lasting effect on the day-to-day life of a person and the *Special Educational Needs Code of Practice* (DfEE, 2001) categorised such pupils according to the amount of support they require. Since 2003 there has been a steady decline in pupils with a Statement of Special Educational Needs by 0.3 per cent and it presently stands at 2.7 per cent of the total number of pupils identified as having SEN. Conversely, the number of pupils requiring less intensive support over the same period of time has risen from 14 to 18.2 per cent. Therefore, it is vital that you can support all pupils including those who are affected by a physical, emotional, social or cognitive disability. Consistently, Ofsted reports between 2004 and 2012 have indicated that many schools have poor monitoring of SEN pupils and therefore it is essential that the learning and accurate assessment of these pupils are addressed.

The English education system includes four nationally benchmarked assessments in primary school to which pupils with SEN are also subjected. National test results indicate that pupils with SEN attain less well than pupils without disabilities. As a result of this underachievement, the self-esteem and self-efficacy of the pupil can be affected, leading to the pupil believing that they cannot succeed.

Self-esteem is a psychological term to reflect one's own emotional state; it is a self-judgement or attitude towards the self. It can encompass emotions such as pride, despair or shame and is closely associated with self-consciousness. Self-efficacy can be regarded as the belief in one's own ability to succeed in particular situations, determined by the way in which one thinks, feels and behaves. It is thought to have an impact on a wide range of emotions, from psychological states to motivation, and to affect all areas of life. It is determined by beliefs held that one's choices can affect situations and that one can deal successfully, or not, with life's challenges. Self-efficacy is the self-belief that aids the pupil to successfully complete tasks and reach goals. Whereas pupils with strong self-efficacy view problems as challenges and form a com-mitment to succeed and recover quickly from setbacks, pupils with poor self-efficacy avoid challenges, believing they will fail, focus on their weaknesses and inabilities and quickly lose confidence in them-selves. Unfortunately, poor self-efficacy can develop in early childhood when dealing with experiences, tasks and new situations and can per-sist throughout life.

Therefore, self-efficacy and self-esteem are crucial aspects of suc-cessful learning (Reid, 2005), with pupils with SEN being at much greater risk of developing low self-esteem (Elbaum and Vaughn 2001). Burden (1998) found that the effect of self-efficacy was strongest at the extremes of the achievement range. The relationship between academic achievement and self-esteem is also well acknowledged in documents such as the *Special Educational Needs Code of Practice* (DfEE, 2001), which purports that self-esteem and self-efficacy are essential for learn-ing because they affect general well-being, social interaction and the motivation of the pupil.

The social-emotional needs of the pupil with SEN are as important as their academic needs. Factors such as dietary deficiency and the home and school environments can strongly influence the self-esteem and self-efficacy of pupils with SEN (Frith, 1999). Whereas you can have little impact on pupils' diets or home situations, you can ensure that the school and classroom ethos is supportive and non-judgemental. Strategies such as *Social and Emotional Aspects of Learning* (DfES, 2005) and the *Primary National Strategy* (DCSF, 2004) offer ways in which the social and emotional well-being of the pupil can be addressed so that learning can take place.

Humphrey (2002) supports the fact that self-esteem and self-efficacy are vital for developing self-worth and an eagerness to succeed, and this must be vital for pupils with SEN who have a social, emotional, psychological or physical disability and are there-fore often starting from a lower position than are pupils unaffected in these ways. Nevertheless, the present education system in Eng-land requires you to assess all pupils, record their progress and report the results to colleagues, parents, governors, the local author-ity or central government. It is within this accountability culture that pupils with SEN can be marginalised in the endeavour to achieve better school results. The next section considers first how self-esteem and self-efficacy can be promoted to ensure all pupils achieve and, second, discusses the different ways in which pupils with SEN can be assessed.

Conditions for learning

The place in which a pupil with SEN is educated is an important factor in meeting their additional needs. Many pupils with SEN benefit from safe, structured and predictable environments (Sellman, 2012). It was Maslow in 1943 who first suggested that there were several requisites that had to be secured before human beings are able to learn. His *Hierarchy of Needs* (1943) strongly suggested that people must have not only their physiological needs such as those for food, water, warmth and comfort addressed, but also their social and emotional needs such as feeling part of a team, being valued and respected, before learning can take place. In the twenty-first century, there is evidence of Maslow's research (1943) in strategies such as Assessment for Learning (Assessment Reform Group, 2002) and Social and Emotional Aspects of Learning (DfES, 2005). The research of Black and Wiliam (1998) also strongly suggests that the classroom and school ethos has a significant impact on the self-esteem and self-efficacy of pupils, which in turn affect their learning. This is supported by Peer and Reid (2003) who state that the social-emotional needs of pupils with SEN are as important as their academic needs.

The Assessment for Learning (AFL) strategy (ARG, 2008) builds on evidence and research from scholars such as Black and Wiliam (1998), Clarke (2001) and Peer and Reid (2003), and suggests that there are six prerequisites for good assessments. Assessment should be accurate, linked to National Curriculum levels, fair, reliable, focused and useful in that it is used for continuity through identifying the barriers to learning and the next steps in learning. The AfL strategy emphasises that assessment should be part of a wider manageable system of data collection and not an isolated activity. It particularly highlights that day-to-day assessments should feed into a clear understanding of the pupil's overall achievements and learning profile.

The importance of creating a safe and secure school and classroom environment is particularly important for pupils with SEN as their disability often makes them feel they are not part of the class, especially if they spend much of the time with a support worker such as a Teaching Assistant (TA). This is highlighted by the research of Farrell (2004) and Vincett et al. (2005), which indicates that the presence of a TA in the classroom may result in a 'Velcro' model of support, in which pupils with SEN become dependent on the TA which causes difficulties when they need to be assessed on their own work. The pupil with SEN would look to the support worker for guidance instead of relying on their own knowledge and understanding of the subject or area to be assessed. The more assured and independent pupils with SEN feel, the more likely they are to relax and learn alongside other members of the class. Only when the SEN pupil is learning is there any point in assessing progress. But if assessment is a bolt-on, such as at the end of a unit of work, or through weekly spelling tests, the pupil with SEN is likely to underperform as their emotional state interferes with their thought processes. It is therefore much better to assess learning through incidental observations, outcomes of daily work or participation in group work.

If you can remember your school days or your training in college or university, how worried were you when you sat an exam, such as an A Level or the Key Skills test or when you submitted an assignment? If you can imagine that these concerns are multiplied for pupils who have a disability, then it is possible to understand how important it is to ensure assessment is part of day-to-day activities and linked closely to learning. It is also vital that pupils with SEN receive regular feedback on how they are doing and that this is delivered in a supportive and positive way.

A need for you to assess, monitor and report on the progress of pupils with SEN is integral to the National Curriculum. This is also a particular focus for Ofsted inspections, so perhaps one of the first things you need to do is set clear targets that are SMART – specific, measurable, achievable, realistic and time-related. A key element in identifying pupils with SEN is the discrepancy between their age and their independent learning ability which leads to an adjustment in access to the curriculum.

When assessing pupils with SEN, it is important to consider the whole situation. This means the level of difficulty, the teaching methods used, the type of learning involved, the physical environment and the relationship between you and the pupil and between the pupil and their peer group. It is also important for you to notice how the pupil with SEN approaches the assessment as well as the responses being given. For example, was it an impulsive response or carefully considered? Did the pupil show anxiety or confidence? Did the pupil self-correct? (Westwood, 2007). It is usual for pupils with SEN to have targets relating to their own performance rather than ones set against the abilities of other pupils in the class. The more specific the targets are, the easier it is to measure progress. Pupils with SEN may have a range of targets in addition to those which are academic. It is important to understand that although national targets focus on the core subjects, it is the whole pupil that you are assessing. For example, there may be social targets for pupils with Asperger's Syndrome, behavioural targets for pupils with Attention Deficit Disorder or organisational targets for dyslexic pupils.

There is no evidence to support the belief that assessment enhances learning, and it can have very negative effects on pupils if it is the kind of assessment to which high stakes are attached, such as that which is published. Black and Wiliam (1998) found that assessment that supports learning must involve pupils in assessing their own achievements and setting their own goals. Of course, pupils with SEN may need support in assessing and target setting, particularly if they have low self-esteem and self-efficacy.

With any pupil, in order to assess their progress a baseline needs to be established. This can be developed from advice and information from colleagues, parents and carers, education or health care professionals and your own observation of the pupil in different situations. Once the baseline is set, then targets can be set and monitored. The diversity of educational experiences prior to the Foundation 2 class can make this task more difficult for the teacher of this class than for any other in primary school. There is a particular dilemma relating to young pupils with SEN as it is difficult to know whether a pupil has a learning disability or if the difficulties they have are related to a slower developmental process which is normal for that pupil. Therefore, it is essential that all pupils, particularly those with SEN, are continuously assessed to ensure that their educational needs are being met (Wolfendale, 1994). This may involve a range of professionals such as an educational psychologist.

Multiagency working is key to the Education Health and Care (EHC) plan (DfE, 2014) which aims to bring together professionals from education, health and social care. The difficulty with this is that it is not a new concept, being first introduced shortly after the Second World War, and developing into the National Children's Bureau in 1963. It was proposed by Warnock in 1978 and was the essence of Every Child Matters (DfES, 2003), which, following the tragic death of Victoria Climbié, was hailed as one of the most important policy initiatives and development programmes in relation to children and children's services. There is a difficulty in gathering together several professionals from different disciplines, even for pupils with Statements of SEN, who are required to have an annual review with all stakeholders present. Therefore, assessing the learning needs of pupils without Statements of SEN lies mainly in your hands, as the teacher. You will of course have the support of the Special Educational Needs Coordinator (SENCo) who can support you in assessing the needs of pupils and developing a learning plan for them. However, in primary school, it is usual for the SENCo to also be a class teacher and therefore the bulk of the assessment, teaching and monitoring will be in your hands. This can take various forms, depending on the age and developmental stage of the pupil and on which subject you are assessing.

Any assessment should be carried out in the context of the normal learning environment of the pupil so that there can also be an assessment of the effect of the physical environment on the learning of the pupil with SEN. It is important that you assess the impact of your provision, the effect of your teaching, whether you are offering equal access to the curriculum for all pupils and the changes to any of these you may need to make. The assessment cycle is perhaps more important for pupils with SEN as they will usually make smaller steps in progress than will pupils without a disability. The *SEN Code of Practice* (DfEE, 2001) promotes the early identification of pupils with SEN and an appropriate intervention being employed to address the learning needs detailed in an Individual Education or Behavioural Plan (IEP/ IBP). These set small SMART targets, and it falls to you to monitor the progress of pupils with SEN in your class and report back to the SENCo at regular intervals.

The use of differentiation in primary classrooms may not always specifically address the learning needs of pupils with SEN and this needs careful monitoring. Differentiation is bound up with content, processes and structure relating specifically to the National Curriculum but rarely relates to other aspects of pupils' development. Differentiation is also difficult if the government and Ofsted promote whole-class teaching (Clough, 1998), as is suggested in the Primary Curriculum 2014.

Similarly, although the tables in many primary classrooms are arranged in groups and collaborative working is thought to develop independent learning, it is easier for pupils to mask their learning difficulties. In fact, Alexander et al. (1992) suggest that in a class of 30 pupils, the support of each pupil is so brief and superficial that it cannot meet the aims of assessing pupils or gathering data on their understanding. Similarly, the more time you spend with one pupil or group of pupils, the less time you have for others in the class. However, where learning is genuinely collaborative, pupils use their peers for support and the increased interactions result in enhanced learning. Moreover, collaborative group work can develop acceptance, a supportive attitude and an understanding of different learning needs, all vital to the pupil with SEN feeling accepted within the class (Wolfendale, 1994). But this will not develop without your input in explaining how to share and support each other and without pupils understanding the difference between copying and collaboration.

Modifications to assessment processes for pupils with SEN may include shortening or simplifying a task, offering the pupil more time or support from a Teaching Assistant, or allowing them to present the work in a different format (Topping and Malony, 2005). For example, a pupil who can illustrate the Norman Conquest through artwork may indicate knowledge and understanding of what occurred in the same way as another pupil may evidence it in a written account. In national tests, it is also possible to enlarge the text and response space, reproduce the tests on different coloured paper or employ a scribe and have the instructions read aloud (except for the reading tests).

Within the classroom, for day-to-day tests you may use oral rather than written questioning, allowing the pupil a scribe, offering short breaks or extra time for completion, or employing a range of assessment strategies, some of which are explained in more detail in later chapters in the book. It is also important to consider your feedback, particularly that given to pupils with SEN as they often have low self-esteem and self-efficacy, as discussed earlier in this chapter. Employing formative language rather than summative will support the pupil in understanding what has been done well but will also provide some targets for further work. Grades or marks can often be disheartening to pupils with educational difficulties as they can easily be compared with other pupils, although a great number of comments may also be off-putting. It may be that you can decide on a code to indicate the effort involved and how well the pupil has achieved the learning objectives. But whilst offering pupils with SEN differing assessment and feedback, this must not be at the expense of the other pupils in the class. You must consider whether what you are doing is fair to all pupils whilst allowing pupils with SEN to demonstrate clearly their competence and attainment.

You may be lucky to have a TA to support you in the classroom and research supports the fact that most TAs support pupils with SEN (Siraj-Blatchford et al., 2004; Thornton and Hedges., 2006; Lowe et al., 2009; Woods et al., 2009), despite them usually being untrained to do so. You will need to assist your TA and take responsibility for discussing the nature of the assessment taking place. You need to be aware of the research of Rubie-Davies et al. (2010) who indicated that TAs are more chatty than teachers and often provide pupils with the answers or complete work for them. This research also found that TAs' explanations were more concerned with task completion than with promoting higher levels of pupil thinking, and the researchers concluded that it was not acceptable for TAs to support pupils with SEN.

P scales

Some pupils with SEN will have great difficulty in accessing the National Curriculum and you may struggle with measuring their progress against National Curriculum levels. For these pupils it may be useful to use P scales. P scales provide a national scale for identifying the attainment of pupils with SEN. They comprise a set of attainment descriptors for use with pupils in Key Stages 1–4 who are working below level 1 of the National Curriculum. P scales were specifically developed for use in the assessment and monitoring of attainment and progress of pupils with SEN. They are a set of descriptions for recording the achievement of pupils with SEN who are working towards the first level of the National Curriculum (level 1) and are designed to be used in the same way as National Curriculum levels, identifying the best fit of the level indicators. They can be used for pupils who are severely behind their peers in one or more areas even if they do not have SEN.

The P scales are split into eight different levels with P1 being the lowest and P8 the highest. Level P8 leads into National Curriculum level 1. The performance descriptions for P1 to P3 are not subject-specific across English, maths and science. The descriptions show the range of overall performance that pupils at this level might demonstrate. Levels P1 to P3 describe early learning and conceptual development. Guidelines are provided on developing and planning a curriculum, on developing skills across the curriculum, and on planning, teaching and assessing the National Curriculum subjects at below level 1 of the National Curriculum. The P scale descriptions of attainment indicate the small steps that some pupils make and can be used to demonstrate attainment and to suggest future teaching (Farrell, 2004).

The P scales were first published in 1998 by the Department for Children, Schools and Families (DCSF) and the Qualifications and Curriculum Authority (QCA), and later reviewed in March 2001, in June 2004 and in 2009. Prior to the introduction of P scales, schools used the code 'W' to describe the attainments of pupils working below level 1 of the National Curriculum during the collection of statutory end of Key Stage test results when pupils were aged 7. However, there were limitations in using this method; the code W could not indicate how far below level 1 a pupil had achieved, thus preventing any real measurement of the pupil's ability below level 1. A new system was required to enable teachers to measure attainments and progress more effectively and thus the P scales were developed.

The Centre for Evaluation and Monitoring's P scales system, based at Durham University, was first introduced in 1999 when it was run on behalf of the QCA. However, the QCA discontinued funding for the system after the 2004 cycle and, in response to requests by schools, the Centre for Evaluation and Monitoring (CEM) has since continued to support the system. Since 2005, a number of improvements have been made in response to the feedback that schools have provided. For example, the value-added feedback has been colour-coded to enable teachers to know exactly the extent to which their pupils have progressed relative to similar pupils.

The CEM analyses the P scales assessment data collected from participating schools. Data is collected in the following areas: speaking and listening, reading, writing, using and applying maths, number, shape, space and measures, scientific enquiry, life processes and living things, materials, physical properties, ICT, PSHE and citizenship. This data is then processed and analysed by the Centre to produce individual pupil and school-level feedback. This information is then fed back to schools, where it is used for a range of purposes, including school SEN self-evaluation and target setting.

P scales must only be used when assessing pupils with SEN or those working significantly below age-related expectations, and is statutory when reporting on attainment for pupils who are working below level 1 of the National Curriculum. They can be used at the end of Key Stage 1 (aged 7), Key Stage 2 (aged 11) and Key Stage 3 (aged 14) for reporting teacher assessment in English, maths and science to the Standards and Testing Agency. P scales in other National Curriculum subjects are also used for reporting on teacher assessment to parents.

If a pupil is at P1i–P3ii level in English, then reading, writing, speaking or listening levels would not normally be appropriate. If a pupil is at a level higher than P3ii in English, then separate levels (P4–P8) can be administered in reading, writing, speaking or listening and an overall English level is not expected. This also applies to maths, number, using and applying maths, and shape, space and measures. For science, a single level from P1 to P8 should be given. There may be exceptional circumstances where a pupil is judged to be at P1i–P3ii in English and/or maths but at P4–P8 in a particular element of the subject.

If schools choose to assess children using P scales towards the end of Year 1, you should base such judgements on a review of evidence gathered from everyday teaching and learning. Professional judgement should be used to decide which P scale description best fits a child's performance (DfE, 2013). Pupils will be set a number of tasks in a range of subjects. Valid levels may vary from one subject to another. The tasks are then rated by you using the P scales criteria and pupils are awarded a particular level using your best fit judgements. The P scales assessment provides objective, independent and robust information that can benefit schools in a number of ways, such as in monitoring pupil progress, setting appropriate targets, informing teaching and being used as part of the school's assessment portfolio for school self-evaluation or to present to Ofsted. The feedback provided by the Centre is confidential and is only supplied to the named coordinator at the registering school. It is not supplied to any other external parties and is not designed to inform league tables. When interpreting the P scales, it is important to be flexible. Pupils with SEN show attainment in highly individual ways (QCA, 2005a).

To conclude, if a child has SEN and their EYFS attainment against the EYFS Profile has not been demonstrated at the end of this stage, the school may wish to continue with an early years curriculum to support the child's learning and development. In this case, the EYFSP, rather than P scales, should be used for assessment as it may be suitable for a small number of pupils aged 5.

Points for Reflection

- Education in English primary schools is based on a set of prescriptive assumptions about the way in which pupils develop.
- Pupils with SEN are often thought of in terms of a deficit model – as there being something wrong that needs fixing, rather than in terms of the service model of providing support to aid achievement.
- Many of the principles for assessing pupils with SEN come down to good teaching practice and are applicable to all pupils.

Further Reading

Croll, P. and Moses, D. (2000) *Special Needs in the Primary School: One in Five*. London: Cassell.

Farrell, M. (2012) *New Perspectives in Special Education: Contemporary Philosophical Debates*. Abingdon: Routledge.

Golder, G., Norwich, B. and Bayliss, P. (2005) 'Preparing Teachers to Teach Pupils with Special Educational Needs in More Inclusive Schools', *British Journal of Special Education*, 32(2): 92–9.

(Continued)

(Continued)

Lewis, A. (1991) *Primary Special Needs and the National Curriculum.* London: Routledge.

Norwich, B. and Kent, T. (2002) 'Assessing the Personal and Social Development of Pupils with Special Educational Needs: Wider Lessons for All', *Assessment in Education: Principles, Policy & Practice*, 9(1): 59–80.

CHAPTER 5

LEARNING THROUGH ASSESSMENT

Chapter Objectives

1 To understand the process of learning through assessment
2 To understand the component parts of the Primary National Strategy and their relevance in today's classroom
3 To understand that formative assessment is a part of the Primary National Strategy but not synonymous with Assessment for Learning

Assessment forms part of the current accountability culture where the stakes are high and the word is synonymous with competition (Wragg, 2001). Assessment can be in many forms but there seem to be two purposes: the macro and the micro. On the one hand, the government and local authorities require assessment data to illustrate the progress of schools and to compare school with school – the macro level. On the other, pupils improving in learning and teachers adjusting their teaching, almost a secondary reason for pupils undertaking assessments, takes place at the micro level. Learning through assessment almost flips the assessment purpose on its head to ensure that the pupil and their learning are central to the process.

Learning through assessment is formative assessment where the pupil and teacher gain information on how to extend and improve the learning of the pupil. There is unequivocal evidence that if use is made of assessment data to provide further learning opportunities, then standards will rise (Black et al., 2002). Black et al. (2002) continue to argue that if assessment is not used to promote learning, then competition rather than personal improvement ensues. This has a negative impact on pupils with lower attainment who then believe they do not have the ability to learn, resulting in an increase in the gap between lower and higher achievers. If you work together with your pupils, this will empower them to become more active learners and eventually take more responsibility for their learning.

Many assessment-focused initiatives, all aimed at increasing educational standards, have been introduced into schools over the last few years, as discussed earlier in this book. Assessment can have a strong effect on the lives of pupils as decisions made by you as teacher, your school, local authority or government can influence the prospects and future opportunities of your pupils. Pupils' work is assessed in many forms, from internal, informal records of progress to high-stakes national tests. When tests pervade the ethos of the classroom and teaching methods focus on the requirements of the test, they will be more highly regarded than what has been learnt. This may well affect the self-esteem of some pupils, such as lower achievers or girls who generally have more test anxiety than boys and are more likely to think the source of success or failure lies within themselves (ARG, 2002b, 2003). Additionally, those pupils whose strengths lie outside the subjects being tested may have a low opinion of their capabilities. The Assessment Reform Group review (ARG, 2002b) suggests that the negative impact of testing on motivation can be avoided if teachers encourage pupils to take responsibility for their own learning, judge their own work against the criteria provided and value their effort and achievements.

The integration of assessment into teaching and the identification of where pupils are in their learning, where they could be and how to get there is the fundamental basis of improvement and progress (ARG, 2008). The Assessment Reform Group proposes a set of broad principles that they suggest should form the basis of any assessment process. The central point is that all assessment should improve learning. Assessments should also be reliable, valid and fit for purpose so that all stakeholders have a clear understanding of the learning goals relevant to pupils' current and future lives. Finally, assessments should vary in form and promote the active engagement of pupils in their learning which will serve to increase the motivation of pupils to evidence their progress and development.

The work of the Assessment Reform Group in the late 1990s and early twenty-first century concluded, after extensive research, that assessment processes within schools could be vastly improved. Their publication in 2002, *Assessment for Learning: 10 Principles* (ARG, 2002a), summarises the key features of Assessment for Learning (AfL) and proposed that it should be a natural, integral and essential part of everyday learning and teaching and a key element of personalised learning. Effective assessment is a way in which the understanding of pupils' learning gained through assessment and reflection can be used to evaluate and enrich the curriculum offered. At its simplest, assessment can be thought of as a three-stage process: (i) gather the evidence which (ii) informs judgements which (iii) leads to outcomes (Drummond, 2003). But AfL is a cyclical process, as seen in Figure 5.1.

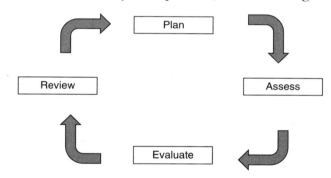

Figure 5.1 The cyclical nature of assessment

Vygotsky (1978) also argued that assessment should be an ongoing process where each new cycle is a new beginning in the learning process and this is the essence of AfL, as opposed to assessment of learning which is what Drummond (2003) refers to above in the three-stage process of assessment.

In 2002, the Assessment Reform Group proposed that assessment should:

- be part of effective planning
- focus on how pupils learn
- be central to classroom practice
- be a key professional skill
- be sensitive and constructive

- foster motivation
- promote understanding of goals
- help learners know how to improve
- develop the skills of self-assessment
- recognise all achievement. (ARG, 2002c)

Using these principles, the DCSF produced the *Primary National Strategy: Excellence and Enjoyment – Learning and Teaching in the Primary Years* (DCSF, 2004) which contained several books and video tapes which explained and illustrated AfL, all housed in the famous *lunch box*. Although these are somewhat dated publications, the principles of assessment and assessment to promote learning are arguably still of value and importance when assessing pupils today.

The Primary National Strategy (DCSF, 2004) explained that AfL is a responsive, flexible and powerful way of raising standards of education; it is an interactive process whereby teachers and pupils are clear about the learning outcomes of the lesson and where learning is the key topic of conversation. It also involves pupils in taking a much greater part in their learning through asking questions, knowing why they are learning something and how to apply learning and improve performance; it is about pupils having the confidence to take risks in their learning and you, as the teacher, responding to their individual needs through effective questioning and informative feedback. In effect, it is what good teachers have always done rather than it having been a new initiative, a quick fix or a package of add-on strategies. The principles of AfL were that teachers should:

- set high expectations, ensuring every learner has the confidence to succeed
- establish what learners know and build on that
- ensure that the pace and structure of the lesson is challenging and inspiring
- generate a love of learning in each pupil
- ensure that pupils are equal partners in their learning
- develop a range of ways to learn.

In effect, the Primary National Strategy (DCSF, 2004) required teachers to tailor teaching and learning to ensure the best progress was made by every pupil and to motivate pupils in order that together the next steps in their learning could be planned. Assessment for Learning, in essence, is any activity in which the teacher seeks to know and interpret where the pupil is in their learning, where they could be and how best to get there (ARG, 2002a).

The DCSF, when publishing the Primary National Strategy (2004), insisted that it would take at least three years and more probably five or six years for schools to deeply embed the AfL strategies within the school. The Association for Achievement and Improvement through Assessment (AAIA, 2005) suggested that there were clear signs that AfL was working effectively in the classroom: the teacher listens and responds, discusses what pupils are learning and allows them to take responsibility for their own learning. Additionally, pupils are motivated, interested and able to talk about their learning; they are actively involved in their learning and both teacher and pupil work collaboratively to further the learning of the pupil. Pupils understand what good work looks like and receive feedback that informs them of their next steps in the learning process, enables them to reflect on their learning and creates opportunities for them to grow in independence and self-direction.

Most teachers would agree that aiding pupils to become independent, confident and effective learners is the prime aim of teaching and this can be achieved by allowing them to recognise their own strengths and points for development. The atmosphere of a classroom can have a direct impact on how effectively pupils learn (Fautley and Savage, 2008). Creating an ethos and environment where pupils can enjoy and reflect on their learning, in order to extend their learning, underlies all teaching, learning and assessment. Without a positive learning environment, pupils are less likely to feel they can make mistakes or admit to a misunderstanding, whereas if the conditions for learning provide a positive culture, mistakes mean someone has learnt something or will be about to learn something new, which should be a source of celebration rather than derision. Pupils will learn effectively if, as Maslow (1943) suggested, they have their physiological, safety, social and emotional needs met.

Maslow's principles (1943) are the essence of AfL in that it ensures the pupil is in the right frame of mind before beginning to learn. Conditions for learning will not be explored further in this book as its focus is on assessment, but it was important to discuss this briefly as, without a key understanding of the conditions for learning, assessment cannot effectively take place.

Although as a teacher you will understand that the pupil's learning is your priority, there is a danger that some teachers may feel that if the activity has been completed successfully, learning has taken place. However, this is not so. You need to be clear about what the learning should be and have clear aims and objectives specifying what is to be assessed. Therefore, the importance of sharing learning outcomes and success criteria with pupils and their parents cannot be underestimated.

Since Ofsted (1996) required it, it is now common practice to see learning objectives written at the front of or somewhere in the classroom for each lesson of the day, but it is the quality of these objectives that is important. With poorly written or absent learning objectives, pupils are left wondering what it is they should learn, do and achieve during the lesson. It also makes the assessment of pupils' achievement almost impossible for you as the teacher. Pupils have a fundamental right to know what they are to learn and what will be assessed. Research indicates that pupils are more motivated, task orientated and focused if they know the learning objective of the lesson and what they need to do to achieve this. Writing learning objectives, though, is not an easy task. They should of course be derived from the programmes of study in the *Primary National Curriculum* (DfE, 2014) but this document is written for adult readers and therefore the learning objectives must be made child-friendly before being shared with pupils. Learning objectives should also be explained to pupils so that they know precisely what they have to do. There must also be a clear distinction between the learning objective and the setting or context within which it is placed.

For example, the instruction: *Write how to make a sandwich* does not provide any indication as to how this should be laid out, the expected language to use or what will be assessed at the end of the lesson. However, if the learning objective was: *Using six instructional words explain how to make a sandwich*, then the purpose of the lesson and what will be assessed become clearer. The six instructional words are the objective of the lesson; the context is the sandwich. Contexts can change; learning objectives do not. For example, *Using six instructional words explain how you would* plant mustard and cress seeds on a plate/make a drink of orange cordial/make toast/direct someone to the head teacher's office, and so on. Objectives could be to write a recount (context: a visit to the farm); to write a formal letter (context: a letter of complaint about the proposed supermarket to be built on the playing fields); or to use adjectives in sentences (context: describing the ugly giant in the story *The Big Friendly Giant* by Roald Dahl). Pupils should know exactly what they have to learn and what they need to do to demonstrate their learning. It does not matter whether the lesson begins with the context or the learning objective as long as pupils are clear on what they need to do and how they can demonstrate they have achieved it. The purpose of success criteria is to ensure pupils know exactly what the teacher is going to assess. In the example above, it would be the six instructional words, and therefore the lesson could begin with:

- We are going to think carefully about how we make a sandwich. You are going to tell me how I can make a sandwich for my lunch. You can choose any filling you like – cheese, ham, tuna, marmite, jam … (context).
- In our Big Book this week we were finding words that tell us to do something – they give us instructions – the bossy words. Can anyone remember some of them? They are useful if we want to tell someone how to do something or how to get somewhere (context).
- Can you think how you would use some bossy words to tell me how to make my sandwich?
- I want you to use six or more bossy words in your writing (learning objective).
- At the end of the lesson I am looking for the six or more bossy words in your writing (success criteria).

The context is explained, the learning is linked to previous knowledge and the learning objective is explained along with the success criteria – how will the pupil and teacher know if the learning objective has been achieved? Muddled learning objectives lead to mismatched activities which are very difficult to assess (Clarke, 2005a, b). Learning objectives inform pupils what they are going to learn; the context places the learning in a familiar setting; and the success criteria tell the teacher and pupils what is to be assessed. Some teachers use WALT and WILF to differentiate between the learning objective and the success criteria:

WALT: We are learning to …

and

WILF: What I am looking for is …

If the process of lesson planning is clear, then pupils will be more focused and persevere longer, behaviour will improve as will the quality of the work and, as pupils discuss the task, they will become more reflective and self-evaluative. Additionally, the assessment of pupils becomes much clearer and simpler. As pupils, or as you as the teacher, become more familiar with this process, the pupils may take a fuller part in the process, such as deciding on the success criteria and assessing whether they have achieved the learning outcomes. The importance of learning outcomes and success criteria is explored again in the chapter on self- and peer assessment (Chapter 6).

Closely linked with learning outcomes and success criteria is setting and using curricular targets, which is a further aspect of the Primary National Strategy (DCSF, 2004).

Curricular targets are based on learning outcomes, informed by an analysis of pupils' work, in discussion with pupils and ideally also with parents or carers. They reflect whole-school priorities identified in the school development and improvement plan and also link with your performance management targets. Historically, targets were set within the school improvement context to focus attention on particular areas of the curriculum. More recently, the government has set national targets for the number of pupils aged 11 who attain level 4 in their English and maths SATs. Although SATs results do not affect pupils themselves, many now speak of them as though there is a personal consequence for attaining a certain level. Research on providing grades and marks for pupils indicates that such pupils are less motivated when compared with other pupils (Clarke, 2001).

Curricular targets are translated into year group targets and then filtered down to group or individual targets within each class. Making pupils aware of these targets helps them recognise how well they are doing and what they need to do next in order to progress in their learning. This process is usually well established in most schools and the focus is often on English and maths, except perhaps in early years settings where targets also focus on the personal, social and emotional aspects of learning. Once targets have been set, you will need to amend the medium- and short-term planning to reflect the challenge of the new targets.

There are three elements to target setting at the pupil level: quantitative tracking of numerical targets annually; qualitative targets that are written; and targets that are not recorded (Clarke, 2001). Most schools have a computer program that monitors pupils' levels of attainment annually and that may include additional data such as whether pupils have free school meals, and their gender and ethnicity, so that a more intensive analysis can take place. The use of ICT in data collection and the curriculum is explored in more depth in Chapter 10. Qualitative data is collected often within the classroom by you as the teacher, having noted the attainment of a pupil through, for example, the explanation of a science experiment or, within the foundation subjects, perhaps an illustration of how the Victorians dressed, or a strengthening of the corners of a structure in technology. Non-recorded targets may be those that are set by pupils for their own purpose following a marked piece of work or after chatting with peers or from the evaluation of how they performed within a certain lesson.

Targets are most effectively set from assessment data that are gathered from lesson evaluations or pupils' marked work or linked directly to the learning outcomes and success criteria of each lesson. Targets will be set at the review stage following an assessment and feed directly into the planning stage that follows. They can also be gathered from a range of day-to-day assessment strategies which is the fourth aspect of the Primary National Strategy (DCSF, 2004) which focuses on AfL.

An assessment activity aids learning if it provides feedback so that you can modify the teaching and learning activities, allowing pupils to move forward in their learning. Previous sections of this book have focused on national and international tests in which primary pupils take part. Day-to-day assessment is that which takes place many times throughout the day and is used primarily for you to adapt your teaching strategies. It involves you monitoring, observing and engaging with pupils throughout each lesson to ensure maximum learning is taking place. For the assessments to have the greatest impact, it is valuable for you to engage pupils in assessing their own work. In order for this to work effectively, it is paramount that the learning outcome is clear and unambiguous, as discussed earlier in this chapter. Discussions with pupils throughout the lesson will provide evidence for instant feedback that should ensure the pupil is on the correct track to achieve the learning outcomes. Day-to-day assessment practices can include questioning and observing, both of which are explored in more depth in future chapters, plus discussion, review and mini-plenaries, all of which take place throughout the lesson. Additionally, you may be able to enrol a TA to either track the progress of an individual or group of pupils or alternatively provide a general evaluation of the whole-class response to learning.

There are a range of quick-fire techniques from which you can choose, some of which are detailed below. You may adapt and add to each of these to ensure they are relevant and appropriate to the pupils you are teaching and the time of day, day of the week or season in the year.

The next few ideas can be used as self-assessment, peer assessment or mini-plenaries throughout the lesson or can be adapted to be a more detailed assessment towards the end of the lesson. All depend on the accurate and honest evaluation of pupils' own or others' work and success rests heavily on the clear and explicit learning outcomes and success criteria set out at the beginning of the lesson. Pupils who are not used to these systems may need practice in order to achieve effective appraisals of their learning. The following examples rely on colour coding in a

Traffic lights   **Thumbs up/down/neither**

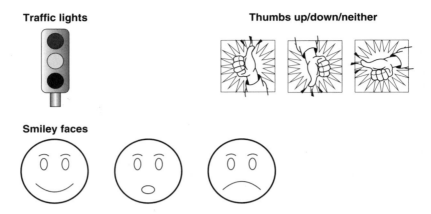

Smiley faces

Coloured cards of different shapes operating as traffic lights, using just colours or words or a combination of both:

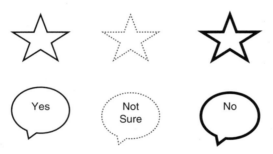

Figure 5.2   Self-assessment ideas

traffic light system: red is for I do not understand/I have not done it; amber is for I think I understand/I may need more practice/I think I have done it; and green is for I have done it/I do understand/I need to move on from this.

You can also use coloured Post-its or have coloured baskets in which pupils place their books or work at the end of the lesson.

Other ways in which pairs or groups of pupils could self- or peer assess are:

Talking partners   <u>Think</u> (on your own), <u>pair</u> (talk with a partner), <u>share</u> with the class

Perhaps a more adventurous but very effective assessment technique for older pupils is snowballing. Despite the excitement it may generate, the pupils are moving out of their seats and actively learning. Each pupil has a piece of paper and the pupils write one thing on the paper, screw it up into a ball and, on your command, throw it somewhere in the room. Pupils then collect one snowball and the process starts again.

This can be effective at the start of, mid-way through or at the end of a unit of work. For example, pupils may write one thing they know about Henry VIII; they then make and throw a snowball; and then the next person writes a different fact they know about Henry VIII. After four or five rounds, the pupils will have several different facts about Henry VIII. These can be used within a group, for example, to generate a fact file or poster about Henry VIII, gathered as a class to create a display or initiate further discussion about this era in history or used individually to start a project on Henry VIII and the Tudor period.

Many different forms or adaptations of the above can be of great use within a lesson to check the ongoing knowledge and understanding of pupils so that the rest of the lesson can be tailored to their continuing learning needs. The more exciting the assessment, the less pupils feel they are being assessed and, in consequence, the more accurate the assessment data will be.

Assessment in conjunction with parents is most prevalent in the early years and tends to reduce as pupils get older. However, parents can provide a wealth of valuable information that may not be available or noticeable in the classroom – for example, the death or illness of a grandparent, sibling, friend or pet; their dad posted to a forces base overseas; or separation of their parents. Therefore, involving parents in the education of their children is a vital component of the Primary National Strategy (DCSF, 2004) and still retains that importance in schools in the twenty-first century.

Working with parents

Parents are usually the first educators of their children long before they arrive in school aged 4 or 5 and therefore know and understand their children far better than anyone else. In fact, throughout primary school pupils spend more of their time at home than in school so parents have an immense part to play in the education of their offspring. Parents should therefore be seen as co-educators and there should be a two-way information flow between you and them. Assessment of Learning, concerned with parental involvement, involves them sharing information with you about their child's interests, strengths and needs. This aids you in the planning and assessment of learning opportunities that will stimulate, interest and extend the pupil's learning. Equally, sharing the learning goals of the pupil with parents and offering ways in which they can support their children at home builds on pupils' learning at school.

Some schools offer half-day sessions where parents can visit the classroom and work with you to deliver lessons. It is a particularly powerful way in which parents can learn about teaching, learning and assessment strategies such as the use of learning outcomes, self-assessment strategies and plenary sessions, in addition to observing how their children react to the learning in the classroom. Of course, such parental involvement needs to be well planned and parents need to be clear on their role within the classroom. This approach provides an opportunity for parents to understand how modern schools operate and may break down barriers, calm fears and reach distant parents who rarely enter the school grounds. The positive from such parental involvement is that pupils can see the benefits of joint teaching, learning and assessment between you and their parents, and, as the confidence of parents grows, they will gain a greater awareness of the value of the learning process and strategies to support their children.

There are many other ways in which parents can play a greater part in their children's education, apart from being in the classroom. These include information evenings for curriculum, assessment, school trip or administrative issues; workshops to explain the ways in which you teach phonics, long multiplication, and so on; book days offering refreshments when parents arrive, collect their children and choose a book together; summer and Christmas fairs; or birthday assemblies, awards assemblies or transition meetings from class to class. National events can also provide opportunities for parents to work alongside you – for example, the Olympic or Commonwealth Games, Red Nose Day, Children in Need, and so on. There are endless opportunities throughout the year to invite parents to join in celebrations or be informed of changes and updates to education, as well as to offer to support their children in the classroom. What research suggests is that the stronger the partnership between parents and teacher, the more settled, conscientious and hardworking the pupil will be in becoming increasingly responsible for their learning.

A further way in which parents can be involved is to be regularly informed of the results of assessments, and, in this light, it is important for you to ensure that you can use the summative data formatively. This is the penultimate area in the *Primary National Strategy* (DCSF, 2004) that is still appropriate in today's schools.

Primary schools have long collected a range of summative test results on reading ages, phonic and spelling knowledge, use of mathematical strategies and other areas of learning, all of which provide a concise view of different aspects of the curriculum. Formative use of summative data can be formulated by pupils through reflection on how they performed and by you as the teacher by examining the results of individuals, groups or the whole class. However it is executed, it entails building on the results of summative tests to analyse the strengths and areas for development that can inform future teaching. In particular, the SATs teacher booklets indicate what types of questions have been asked and these can therefore be applied to the rest of the scripts to elicit whether the errors were made by individuals or can provide a future teaching point that needs to be addressed. Additionally, dialogue with pupils can provide information on their thought processes as they approached the summative tests. Further ways in which pupils can be involved in using summative data formatively is for you to support and structure their revision or for pupils to engage in peer and self-evaluation, and there may be other ways in which the summative data can positively affect future teaching and learning.

School-level data is collected through national tests and provides an indication of how well your school is performing against similar schools locally and nationally and compared with the top-performing schools regionally and nationally. These are completed at certain points in pupils' education, notably at ages 5, 6, 7 and 11. Intelligent use of data from these tests can offer information on how well pupils are performing against a range of criteria, including comparisons of pupils' gender and ethnicity, and those with free school meals and SEN, highlighting areas for development in your school. One warning that must be heeded is that if your school is small, percentages may affect the overall percentages so care must be taken when analysing the raw data.

There are also computer-based programs that will provide an indication of individual pupils' progress in specific areas of the curriculum which will be considered later in this book (in Chapter 10). These programs can track individual pupils' progress throughout primary school and provide predictions for pupils aged 11 based on their performance at age 7. Similarly, there are optional tests for pupils aged 8, 9 and 10 which can be used to identify strengths and weaknesses of individuals, groups and whole classes, which should lead to adaptations of the teaching and learning strategies accordingly.

All summative tests can provide a benchmark for each pupil from which future progress can be judged. By monitoring the progress of individuals, a profile can emerge of each pupil's strengths and areas for development which can also have an impact on the effectiveness of teaching and learning. Whereas summative tests in themselves cannot raise standards, using them formatively can pinpoint specific areas for development which can be particularly effective in raising standards of education for individual, group and whole-class groups.

Most summative tests only exist for the core subjects of English, maths and sometimes science, although there are many more subjects in the primary curriculum that should also be assessed. For example, without assessment you would not know if a pupil understands the differences between ways of life at different times in history or why places are similar to and different from other places in the same country or elsewhere in the world. It is your responsibility to provide an indication to parents at least once per year of the progress of their children in all primary curriculum subjects, as without this you will be unable to assess the progress of pupils in the foundation subjects.

In the humanities, it may be that subjects such as history, geography and religious education are taught as discrete subjects or in combination. Either way, there is a wealth of knowledge and understanding involved such as map reading, using artefacts, attitudes and values to be assessed which will involve a wide and varied approach. It may be that some knowledge is personal, such as that in religious education, or contentious, such as pollution, green sources of energy or conservation. Similarly, there may be a mixture of facts and opinions or attitudes that need to be assessed. Whilst some values will be difficult to assess, if well-argued and tenable they will become easier to appraise. Ways in which the humanities may be assessed include discussion and debate, drama such as hot seating, project work and presentation, posters, illustrations and models. Varying the assessment type for different subjects, depending on what you want to evaluate, is important to ensure pupils remain engaged. Additionally, for children with SEN, a variety of assessments in the National Curriculum subjects could provide an opportunity for pupils to excel in achievement, as discussed in the previous chapter.

In the expressive arts, such as technology, art, music, physical education, dance and drama, it has become more usual for criterion-referenced assessment to take place in which both formative and summative data are collected (Wragg, 2001). This may be, for example, in technology where the process of making the chair is as important as the final product, for example, the completed chair. Similarly, it may be the process of continual refinement of a dance or knowledge of stage directions in a drama that an individual or group is assessed on in addition to the final production. In music, there is debate as to whether assessment should focus on the impact of the final piece or on individual interpretation, rhythm or tempo. Therefore, it is important for you to consider closely the requirements of the primary curriculum and base your assessments on this.

Finally, the Assessment for Learning strategy (DCSF, 2008), an update of the Primary National Strategy (DCSF, 2004), highlights four aims:

- All pupils know how they are doing and how to improve.
- All teachers can assess effectively and plan for the future progression of all pupils.
- All schools have a robust assessment system that is manageable and tracks pupil progress accurately.
- All parents/carers are regularly informed of how well their child is progressing and of the support they can provide to enhance learning.

These four principles are the essence and core of learning through assessment. If you, as a teacher, can adhere to these principles, then the standards of all pupils will rise.

 Points for Reflection

- Which parts of the Primary National Strategy can I evidence in my classroom?
- Which parts of the Primary National Strategy would I like to improve?
- Formative assessment is not synonymous with Assessment for Learning but is a part of it.
- How clear are my learning objectives? Is the context separate? How easily can I assess the success criteria?
- How involved are the pupils in my class in their learning and assessment? Could this be improved?

 Further Reading

Bandura, R. (1997) *Self-Efficacy: The Exercise of Control*. New York: Freeman and Co.

Chapman, C. and King, R. (2005) *Differentiated Assessment Strategies: One Tool Doesn't Fit All*. Thousand Oaks, CA: SAGE.

Gardner, J. (2011) *Assessment and Learning*. London: SAGE.

Goleman, D. (1998) *Working with Emotional Intelligence*. New York: Bantam Books.

Harlen, W. and Gardner, J. (2006) *The Role of Assessment in Developing Motivation for Learning*. London: SAGE.

CHAPTER 6

SELF- AND PEER ASSESSMENT

Chapter Objectives

1 To learn a range of strategies to improve the effectiveness of self- and peer assessment
2 To understand how explicit learning objectives and success criteria are essential for effective self- and peer assessment
3 To understand how self-assessment and peer assessment increase motivation and enhance learning for both the assessor and the assessed

In the past, assessment was something that was done to pupils by teachers and involving pupils in the evaluation of their own and other pupils' learning would have been an alien thought. In the latter half of the 20th century, involving pupils in their learning and assessment became more common and by the 1990s, when the Assessment Reform Group was commissioned by the government of the time to comment on the state and impact of assessment in primary and secondary schools, involving pupils in learning and assessment was increasingly promoted in research and literature. There are both practical and fundamental reasons why pupils should be involved in assessment. Practically, if pupils can be involved in their own assessment and learning, it reduces the responsibility of the teacher in this area. Fundamentally, it will change the dynamics between teacher and pupil, where the pupil takes more responsibility and the teacher relinquishes some. This may cause a problem in that research suggests that the summative tests pupils complete during their primary years give them a negative attitude towards assessment in general, and other studies indicate that many primary pupils believe that assessments are for the school or their parents and cannot see the link with their learning (Crooks, 1988; Butt, 2010). Additionally, less able pupils believe the purpose of assessments is to make them work harder.

In a study of pupils from age 5 to 9, researchers asked the pupils to rank their ability within the class. The results indicated that pupils' perceptions matched incredibly closely the teacher ranking, which implies that even very young children can assess their teacher's perception of them and their peers (Crocker and Cheeseman, 1988). In essence, many pupils find it difficult to transfer from norm-referenced to criterion-referenced thinking. This means that they see the purpose of assessment as a comparison with other pupils, which, for less able pupils, results in de-motivation and the most able pupils failing to be challenged. Criterion-referenced thinking involves pupils setting targets for themselves, assessing their own development against their past assessments and setting future targets for their next challenge. It is pupils challenging themselves, not comparing themselves with other pupils. Criterion-referenced thinking is essential for both self- and peer assessment, but switching to this way of thinking can be difficult for some pupils, especially the less able.

If pupils cannot grasp the purpose of their learning and relate this to assessment criteria, they will be unable to assess their own learning. What is perhaps more worrying is that young children are already forming opinions as to whether they will succeed or not. More able pupils tend to be motivated to learn, will persevere with difficulties and are confident of their success, whilst the less able pupil will experience the opposite of these qualities. In order to understand how assessment affects pupils, it is necessary to be aware that, in general, younger pupils are more motivated than older pupils and much rests on the self-esteem and self-efficacy of the individual; this in turn is affected by responses given by you as the teacher to their assessments. Therefore, there is a need for a positive learning environment to foster high self-efficacy so that self-assessment can take place.

Much research (Butt, 2010) in the twenty-first century indicates the significant progress made by pupils who engage with self-assessment, and if the self-assessment is linked directly with the learning outcomes and success criteria of the lesson, then pupil progress, motivation and self-esteem are all increased. For pupils to play an equal part in their learning, it is essential that they have a secure understanding of the assessment and of your expectations. This will allow the pupil to become more autonomous in gaining a self-awareness of their own work and to monitor it throughout the process to the finished product. Assessment should not be purely summative but a two-way process in which both teacher and pupil are involved in using assessment to promote future learning. Teaching, learning and assessment are undoubtedly interlinked and it is almost impossible to separate them or leave one aside. The role of pupils in this process is vital as they can provide insight into their own learning that no one else can.

Self- and peer assessment have a unique impact on pupils' learning which cannot be accomplished in any other way (Black et al., 2003) and if such assessment is a holistic element of your teaching, then it will infiltrate all parts of your lesson. Effective assessment rests on the situation and the pupils themselves. It depends on the context in which the feedback is given and whether the pupil is ready to receive and trust what is being said (Butt, 2010). In a study by Black and Wiliam (1998), schools that employed self- and peer assessment strategies had a mean gain of twice the control group, which indicates the huge positive impact these strategies can have on pupils' learning.

Logically, how the work was executed, the difficulty of the task and assessment of the resulting work are best placed with pupils; you can often only assess the finished article, not the process of learning that was involved in getting there. Valuable assessment provides opportunities to build on prior learning and extend future learning. Self-/peer assessment is neither a quick fix to reduce teacher marking nor a replacement for teacher marking and feedback. It is not an addition to teacher assessment but is part of the whole process that strengthens the link between teaching, learning and assessment. It engages pupils in effectively assessing their own learning and in becoming self-critical and independent learners. Your role in this will be to oversee the process, moderating the feedback to ensure it is a fair representation. It involves pupils understanding the learning process, where they are in their learning and where they want to be and identifying the next steps in getting there; pupils are involved in the analysis of their own and others' work. Self-/peer assessment is a collaborative strategy whereby the pupil has ownership and responsibility for their own learning. It is a reflective activity and can be written or oral in nature and can be carried out at any point during the lesson, not just at the end of it. In fact, if the process of self-/peer assessment was initiated part way through the lesson, it would offer time for the assessed pupil to improve their work by acting on the suggestions made.

It is important when initiating either self- or peer assessment to set clear boundaries, behaviours and expectations, such as listening skills, taking turns and collaboration, to ensure the process is productive and effective. Pupils may need considerable help in developing self- and peer assessment. For example, it may be necessary to support those pupils who are less able to communicate, those who take criticism badly, those with SEN or with English as an additional language, and those who are too candid in their comments. Discussions with pupils will offer ideas on what works well and what does not. Pupils like to work within structures so it may be possible for you to draw up some dos and don'ts to support their feedback. If they are used to working with *three stars and a wish*, this may be a strategy that can be developed further within self- and peer assessment.

Children learn easily from each other in all aspects of life so extending this into the classroom may at first be alien as the pupils seem to be taking over some of the teacher's responsibilities, but such assessment can provide immense opportunities for deep learning. If self- and peer assessment work well, there should be no need for anyone else to assess the pupils (Brown et al., 1996). Of course, this is quite a radical view as assessments are required as a summative judgement of where the pupil is in their learning at four times during their primary years and it would be unthinkable that you as the teacher would play no part in the assessment process. The Assessment Reform Group (2002a) suggested that teachers should equip pupils with the skills to become independent and take control of their learning. They continue to state that independent learners have an ability to engage in self-reflection and therefore identify the next steps in their learning and consequently acquire new learning and new skills. This is the essence of self- and peer assessment.

Self-assessment

Self-assessment is the process of pupils evaluating their own work and is an inherently valuable learning experience for the pupil involved as it develops empowerment and independence as a learner. Self-assessment skills are not only a valuable strategy for raising attainment in the classroom but they are also useful in pupils' future lives as it is a reflective nature that underpins many vocational and academic courses. It was one of the strategies first introduced by Black and Wiliam (1998), who reported that pupils as young as 5 years old were successfully employing self-assessment strategies, comparing their present performance with earlier versions and then looking forward to what should be accomplished next. Essentially, self-assessment is an ipsative process whereby the pupil reflects on the learning that has taken place, on the work that has been produced and on the next steps in the learning process; this is a cyclical progression. If pupils are truly involved in an appraisal of themselves, then the resulting evaluation is self-assessment that involves future learning. This was highlighted in research by Ross et al. in 1993 who asked pupils to appraise their own artwork, and by Darling-Hammond et al. in 1995 in the USA whose pupils were required to present a report on their learning each year to teachers, other pupils and parents. Both studies found that pupils were insightful, providing a rich and sophisticated account that included their future learning goals. This research suggests that if pupils are to become effective learners, they need to develop as thinkers in their understanding of how to improve from the assessment results gathered; self-assessment is fundamental to future learning (Black, 1998). Ideally, assessment activities should be built into the learning process whereby pupils can assess their knowledge, understanding and skills at various times and have a chance to repeat assessments if they wish in order to improve their performance. The capacity of pupils to assess their own work as part of formative assessment is an integral part and powerful source of learning (Black, 1998). Self-assessment relies on pupils understanding how they learn, and developing as an effective learner is closely linked to personal development as a whole (Black, 1993). It is the pupil's feelings about their learning and assessment that are key to successfully developing self-assessment strategies that include mapping the way forward.

There are various forms of self-assessment, from a review of progress to a reflective account of what happened, or a full evaluation of pupils' work providing suggestions on how to improve. It is interlinked with learning where the pupil is the driver in that learning. As Black et al. (2003) explained, it is almost impossible for a pupil to attain a learning goal if they do not know the essence of that learning goal nor understand how to reach it, and therefore self-evaluation is an essential part of learning. A vital aspect of self-assessment is that pupils should be clear about what exactly they are learning through explicit learning outcomes and success criteria being set at the start of the lesson. If expectations are transparent and explicit, then pupils will understand what it is they have to do and what will be assessed at the end of the lesson. Without having a clear concept of the activity to be completed and the standards expected, pupils will be unable to effectively assess their learning.

Research supports the fact that through self-assessment pupils become more committed and reflective learners (Weeden et al., 2002). Self-assessment is the process whereby the pupil reflects on and remembers their past experiences and draws on these to extend their learning. Although you are in control, pupils endorse what they are to learn. They are in control of the organisation of the resources needed to successfully complete their learning. They record how they think they did and, together with you, agree actions for future learning. Self-assessment involves a range of teaching strategies which can be used in many learning situations, although it essentially involves you relinquishing some control of the pupils' learning. This of course has an impact on the power differentials in the classroom and the traditional roles of teacher and pupil. Therefore, adopting self-assessment strategies requires pupils, teachers and parents to adapt to change.

Many teachers have employed review sessions in their classrooms, asking pupils questions such as how hard they thought they worked or whether they found the work difficult. But pupils generally have little knowledge of the requirements of the National Curriculum or the expectations of national tests. Therefore, although self-assessment removes part of your role, there are clearly aspects that you, as the teacher, need to lead and control. As pupils take increasing control of their learning, there is a shift from the traditional to the collaborative, with pupils gaining in responsibility and independence. The essence of any assessment is to narrow the gap between what pupils know and what they ought to know, as directed by the National Curriculum. It is the pupils themselves that need to work towards closing that gap in order to move forward in their learning, and self-assessment can provide them with the information needed and a better understanding of how to narrow that gap.

Pupils need practice in evaluating their own work so it may be advisable for them to practise with Post-it notes. For example, they could write down six qualities or skills they have, one on each Post-it, then rank them in order from the most important to the least. Pupils will need a lot of support to effectively assess their own performances when self-assessment is first introduced. This support can be gradually withdrawn the more skilled pupils become.

All pupils benefit from self-assessment although pupils with higher attainment seem to find it easier to employ the strategies than do less able pupils. Perhaps one of the hardest things that pupils need to do to be successful with self-assessment is to think of their learning as a set of goals. Similarly, the ability to set realistic, challenging, focused and achievable targets and meet those goals within a reasonable time frame is a further difficulty when introducing self-assessment as a learning strategy. Additionally, some pupils are hard on themselves, destroying their own self-esteem, and some may find it debilitating as their failures are highlighted. Other pupils may be afraid of failure and therefore it is essential that self-assessment has a positive effect on pupils, being introduced and monitored sensitively and considerately. Nevertheless, all pupils need to be taught how to effectively self-assess. One way in which this can be done is to increase the meta-cognitive skills of pupils so that they understand how they learn best. Essentially, it is about asking questions such as: How do I work best? What have I learned? How well did I do it? How could I do it better in the future? Another way is to provide a structure or checklist to support the thinking process. If pupils are allowed time to think, they will learn more effectively as they evaluate what they have learnt and consider how to improve. Generally, older pupils are more self-aware and find less difficulty in responding to such questions but by nurturing these skills in younger pupils it will set them up for more effective learning as they grow older.

Self-assessment is a skill to be learnt and some pupils will inevitably find this harder than others as they may feel other pupils are judging their success. But it is important for you to stress that self-assessment is ipsative and pupils will need to continually reflect on their own prior learning in order to move forward. Self-assessment is an evaluation of the progress made by the individual pupil and pupils compare themselves with themselves rather than against the performance of other pupils, which allows them to become advocates of their own learning and success.

Whereas there is a definite link between learning, teaching and assessment, Airasian (1991) suggests that in self-assessment these are almost indistinguishable as they merge into one another. Merging assessment with the learning process makes it support and motivate rather than a daunting thing that the teacher does at the end of the lesson. Therefore, self-assessment can increase motivation to learn as it allows pupils to share information with you as their teacher and therefore take a positive role in the decisions taken about their learning; a more motivated learner, learns more and achieves higher results.

Generally, pupils' self-assessment is reliable and trustworthy although this is more likely if learning outcomes and success criteria are overt and unambiguous. It is also important that pupils are supported in how to assess and what comment to make. Therefore, previously assessed pieces of work can be used as examples, providing an opportunity for teachers and pupils to learn from the different comments written. Other ways in which pupils can be aided in effective self-assessment is by discussing the possibilities in a pair or in a group, looking at a resource or book to ascertain its main aims or identifying the purpose of the learning and assessment, setting their own tasks and generating the success criteria from the learning outcomes provided by you as the teacher.

There is a range of ways in which pupils can record their assessment, such as journals, interviews, portfolios, discussion or by employing one of the day-to-day assessment strategies discussed in the previous chapter. It is also important to consider the ethos of the classroom and to develop a no-blame culture by regarding mistakes as learning opportunities. Time for thinking, reflecting, articulating and use of positive body language increase self-esteem and refocus *difficulty* to *something that makes you think*. The less criticism and reproach used, the more assessment will foster confidence and increased self-esteem and self-efficacy in pupils to take on a critical appraisal of their own learning.

Peer assessment

Peer assessment is in essence the same as self-assessment and can have the same impact on pupil performance, although it involves pupils assessing each other's work. It is a pupil-centred approach which is increasingly used as an invaluable way in which pupils are closely involved in the assessment and learning of other pupils' work. It may be daunting at first for pupils to comment on their peers' achievements but it is an ideal way in which pupils learn from each other by identifying where they have gone wrong and offering advice on how to improve.

Peer assessment helps pupils gain a clearer understanding of assessment, identify what they still need to learn and work towards bridging the gap. Therefore, engaging with peer assessment also has a positive impact on self-assessment (Butt, 2010). Peer assessment is effective in that there is a significant increase in the motivation to learn. A further advantage of peer assessment is that it enhances pupils' personal, social and emotional development, their thinking skills and rules of citizenship (Wragg, 2001), as they are required to communicate with their peers in a non-judgemental way. Pupils soon realise that if they want to receive supportive and developmental feedback from others, then they should provide this when they report back to other pupils. Peer assessment involves further perspectives in that the work receives feedback from the teacher, the pupil who did the work and the peer who assesses it. It is also reflective in that pupils who peer-assess also reflect on the successes of their own work and identify strengths and areas for development; it aids both the assessor and assessed in understanding the next step in their learning journey. Additionally, peer assessment helps strengthen the student voice and improves communication between pupils and teacher. This inevitably reduces your workload as pupils are recognising and informing you of their own learning needs. Moreover, as pupils are engaged in peer assessment, it offers you an opportunity to observe and reflect on the peer-assessment process. It also plays an important part in developing a positive classroom environment where the focus is on learning, and making mistakes offers only a learning opportunity, not derision or embarrassment.

Peer assessment works well with presentations by pupils, written work, mathematical calculations, practical work, posters and portfolios but its success depends on how well you have prepared the class in the strategies of peer assessment. It may be best to introduce it slowly, working within a couple of subjects throughout the week. Pupils need to practise linking their feedback closely to the learning outcomes and success criteria for the lesson and learn the style of writing or form of words to use to be supportive and offer developmental feedback. They may practise on previous work, have the process modelled by the teacher or begin by using Post-it notes so that inappropriate feedback can easily be removed.

Modelling and explaining are two effective strategies to illustrate the processes of self-assessment to pupils. By explaining and showing pupils how to assess the learning of other pupils and generate targets for their development, it provides an opportunity for pupils to ask questions and for you to reiterate key points of the process such as the link with the learning outcomes and success criteria of the lesson. Pupils can also be used in the modelling and explaining process which will serve to illustrate to other pupils that it is a strategy they too can use, therefore enhancing their self-efficacy. Assessment of the learning process is typically executed at the end of the lesson, although use of it throughout the lesson proves to be much more effective in addressing and remediating issues immediately. The important point to remember is that pupils' work is central to the assessment and learning process.

Peer assessment needs to be prepared and pupils taught how to respond effectively to other pupils' work. Cooperation and collaboration must be engendered rather than competition which could lead to unfair appraisals of a peer's work. If a supportive culture is generated in the classroom, then pupils' learning will increase. The advantages of peer assessment are that pupils find out that others have similar difficulties to them and this encourages them to say where and with what they need help, to speak about their learning and to set their own targets in conjunction with other pupils. As the focus of peer assessment is positive, you often find out more about future planning than through any other process as it develops pupils' awareness of their learning needs and offers an opportunity for you to see into pupils' minds, how they operate and how they learn.

Some questions for self- and peer assessment

- What have you learnt that is new?
- How do you know you have learnt it?
- What are you most pleased about?
- What made you think the most when you were learning?
- What were the most difficult bits?
- How did you overcome the difficult parts?
- Where did you go for help when something got difficult?
- With what do you still need help?

Based on Clarke (2001)

A thinking time of 20–30 seconds should be allowed for reflection on each question and the answers. All questions should be linked closely to the learning outcomes and success criteria.

The skills of both self-assessment and peer assessment take time to develop, especially with lower attainers who have less confidence and motivation for learning. Initially, when first establishing a self-assessment process in the classroom, it will be teacher-focused as pupils learn how to use the strategy. You have knowledge of the National Curriculum, education practices and assessment requirements, although in time, with practice, much of this will be handed over to pupils as they take more control of their own learning. Starting the process in the early years can help to embed self-assessment into classroom practices and, as pupils progress through school, their self-assessment practices will become more refined. As pupils become more practised in self-assessment, it will free you from excessive marking and being the sole assessor, shifting some of the responsibility for learning on to pupils. As a result, pupils become more engaged and autonomous in their learning, finding solutions for their difficulties rather than simply asking the teacher (Butt, 2010). So, with a little investment of time, pupils' learning is more effective, which not only increases their motivation and successes but may be a more efficient use of time once the strategies are embedded, though it is a long-term process.

Self- and peer assessment can also be used in conjunction with one another. For example, once pupils have self-assessed their own work, they may work in pairs or small groups to justify their judgements. Or, using the traffic light system highlighted in Chapter 5, pupils can indicate if they have understood (green), need a little help (orange) or need much more support (red). The green and orange groups could then each form a group to discuss their learning, whilst the teacher works with those pupils who indicated they need much more assistance in order to understand the lesson. Although this in a way is differentiation, pupils have identified their own learning needs and the teacher is focusing on those who need support. Because the response to the red group is instant and the pupils realise that the focus is on learning not assessment, they gain the confidence to disclose that they need extra help.

For effective self- and peer assessment, the feedback must be instant. The traditional way of the teacher defining the goal, judging the outcome and attempting to close the gap by offering suggestions for improvement that will hopefully be implemented next lesson is flawed. At best, pupils easily forget what has happened last lesson or yesterday and at worst they could ignore the comments teachers make as the work is in the past, it is finished and they cannot or do not want to transfer the knowledge to other learning. Allowing pupils to make instant improvements based on their own or other pupils' comments, by employing self- and peer-assessment strategies, is much more powerful for enhancing learning, increasing motivation and encouraging independent learners. Additionally, research suggests that pupils receive criticism more easily from peers than they do from the teacher, possibly because all pupils have engaged in the same learning so there is a shared understanding of its difficulty or the language used and it is altogether more child-friendly. Pupils who use self- and peer assessment regularly reflect on their work, take pride in their work and modify and improve their work as a natural part of developing their learning in everyday school life.

You may want to place key questions around the room such as: 'What have I learned?', 'What do I think is best?', 'What did I find difficult?' and 'How can I improve next time?' Allowing pupils to take responsibility for aspects of classroom management and organisation encourages independence that leads to motivation and further learning. Discussions between peers can enhance the comments made in both self- and peer assessment through listening to the language used and how effectively the pupil worked, their independence, self-reliance, reflectivity and motivation for learning. Self- and peer assessment is much more effective than you marking the work away from the pupils as it is instant and generated by the pupils themselves. In fact, many reports since the original review of assessment by Black and Wiliam in 1998 strongly suggest that the traditional format of teacher marking using grades or marks and providing feedback with external rewards such as stickers, at worst led to regression of pupils' knowledge, understanding or skills and at best had limited impact. Marking, recording and reporting are further discussed later in this book.

One difficulty you may find when encouraging pupils to engage with self- or peer assessment is moving them away from purely descriptive or unhelpful comments such as: 'You did this well', 'I like your work' or 'I think you worked hard'. Pupils need to be drawn back to the learning outcomes and success criteria for the lesson and make comments using the language of these such as: 'You used six adjectives in your poem', 'You explained clearly why some objects float and some sink', 'Your drawing clearly explains the weather cycle', etc. It important to create a positive, constructive and motivational environment in which the focus is on pupils owning their learning through effective assessment processes that offer developmental suggestions for improvement. It is a good idea when peer marking to ensure that peer-assessment partners are of a similar standard in their learning, to ensure both pupils understand their role and to allow them time to consider and reflect on their responses.

With early years pupils, comments may be oral rather than written and you may want to start the process with the whole class. For example, ask a pupil to self-assess how well they shared the books in the book corner. By asking pertinent questions, self-assessment strategies begin to emerge: 'How well do you think you shared the books in the book corner?', 'How do you know this?', 'What did you do to share?', 'How did you feel when you shared the books with the other pupils?' Taking this further to peer assessment would be to ask someone else in the book corner how well they thought another pupil shared the books. Through asking questions in a whole-class situation, all pupils are hearing the language used for self- and peer assessment which is the basis for future development in these areas.

It is important for pupils of all ages in primary school that self- and peer assessment does not become routine, boring and ineffective. To avoid this, it is wise to use different methods, different groupings and different formats for reporting in different subjects or areas of the curriculum. It is also important that parents understand the processes of self- and peer assessment so that at parents' evening they are not concerned when they observe more feedback from other pupils than you in their child's work.

Finally, be aware that as pupils develop their self- and peer-assessment strategies and become more reflective learners, they may challenge you as the teacher. Pupils may demand that lessons are interesting, motivating and relevant and that your assessment is developmental!

Points for Reflection

- Self-assessment and peer assessment are unique in their ability to raise standards.
- Pupils' self-assessment requires a reflective judgement of their work.
- Peer assessment can improve the learning of both the assessed and the assessor.
- Pupils must be instructed how to self- and peer-assess.
- Pupils can be used to model the processes of self- and peer assessment.
- Pupils can assess themselves if the learning objectives and success criteria of the lesson are clear and unambiguous.
- Self-assessment and peer assessment are fundamental to effective learning.
- Self-assessment and peer assessment are ipsative in that they look back at the learning journey but look forward to bridge the gap between what has been achieved and what can be achieved.
- Self-assessment and peer assessment change the role of pupils and their relationship with the teacher.
- Some key questions can be established to be used by pupils (see above).
- Pupils should be given thinking and reflection time to respond to questions.
- The process can be supported by offering review formats.
- Oral rather than written feedback should be encouraged.
- Pupils can be encouraged to use constructive feedback that provides information on how to improve and bridge the learning gap; aim for a 3:1 ratio of positive–negative feedback.
- You can start by facilitating discussions about assessment.
- Time should be allowed for self-assessment and/or peer assessment to become embedded into the classroom learning process.
- Self-esteem and self-efficacy are key to effective learning and the ability to effectively self- and peer-assess.

Further Reading

Butt, G. (2006) 'Using Assessment to Support Students' Learning', *Into Teaching – the Induction Year*, 1(13): 15–20.

Dix, P. (2010) *The Essential Guide to Classroom Assessment*. Harlow: Pearson.

Falchikov, N. (2005) *Improving Assessment through Student Involvement*. London: Routledge.

Lewis, R. (1984) *How to Help Learners Assess Their Progress*. London: Council for Educational Technology.

Roberts, T.S. (2006) *Self, Peer and Group Assessment in E-learning*. London: Information Science Publishing.

CHAPTER 7

USING OBSERVATIONS AND MIND MAPPING

Chapter Objectives

1 To think differently about assessing pupils
2 To learn about observation techniques to assess pupils' learning
3 To understand the difference between mind maps and concept maps
4 To understand how both mind maps and concept maps can be used as assessment strategies

The following four chapters discuss the merits of several different types of assessment that do not rely on paper tests or worksheets. Being of a more practical nature, they are more inclusive in that writing does not form a barrier to assessing the achievements of pupils. There is no requirement to assess pupils through a written method, except, of course, for evaluating writing.

This chapter is concerned with the use of observations and mind maps to assess pupils' learning.

Observations

Observations are a normal part of the education system, from teacher appraisals and trainee teacher lesson observations to educational psychologists' observations and Ofsted inspections. Formal observation of primary-aged pupils to assess their learning beyond the early years is perhaps still in its infancy, but observation is key to understanding pupils' learning.

Observation as an assessment strategy in primary school is the active surveillance and recording of what pupils do, how they act and react, how they approach tasks and their relationship with other pupils. It is fundamental to your knowledge and understanding of the pupils you teach. This is not a simple task. Black (1998) suggests that observation is difficult because it needs to be intensive in order to provide valid data. However, by observing how pupils behave it can offer you an insight into how pupils learn. It is also difficult because you can only see what is in your own experience, which leads to the possibility of missing vital learning if you have not previously experienced it or you are not particularly looking for it. Additionally, if you are going to remain in the background whilst doing the observation, there is the issue of who is doing the teaching. It may be that you can engage a TA to do the observation whilst you teach the class. However, this has difficulties in that the TA may not gather the information you want, although, on the positive side, different and significant data may have been gathered which you had not considered.

Observation is more prevalent in early years settings, perhaps because of the nature of the curriculum, the ways in which young pupils learn and the fact that adult-to-pupil ratio is required to be higher. This situation is less typically replicated with older pupils in primary school, making observations more difficult to execute.

The idea of observation stems from biologists' observations of animal behaviour and sociologists' anthropological studies of people, referred to as ethnography. Observation in education was first developed by American educational psychologists. This led to information on understanding the development of young children and was the start of McMillan nursery provision in 1928, and this way of teaching young pupils is still popular today.

The first guidance or curriculum for early years pupils in England was published in 1996 although this was replaced in 2012 with the *Statutory Framework for the Early Years Foundation Stage* (DfE, 2012). *Birth to Three Matters* (DfES, 2003) detailed the importance of observation in the development of babies between birth and their third birthday. But observing pupils throughout primary school, not just in early years departments, can still have many benefits as it will help you to understand how primary-aged pupils think, work, communicate and play.

Teachers make hundreds of automatic observations every day and are expert in reading situations from the ways in which pupils react, what they say or their body language. Whereas it is likely that all primary teachers observe noteworthy incidents, behaviours or actions, these may not be recorded at the time, or may be added to pupils' records at a later date. There may be the perception that anecdotal evidence needs to be gathered in early years as this contributes towards judgements of pupils' progress and is recorded in the Early Years Foundation Stage Profile (EYFSP), as discussed earlier in this book. Later in the primary years, the data required tends to be driven more by knowledge and understanding of the National Curriculum programmes of study than by personal, social and emotional development, despite this being part of the primary curriculum. Nevertheless, it may be that the personal portfolio developed in the early years should be continued throughout primary school as a record of the learning journey of the pupil. This links closely with the idea of personal portfolios, which is discussed further in Chapters 9 and 10.

Different observational techniques may be used for different purposes but all can be used as an assessment strategy. Planned observations can be divided into qualitative and quantitative approaches. Qualitative observations gather actions, behaviours, emotions and social interactions and are usually recorded by you with words. Quantitative observations gather numbers such as the frequency of interactions with peers or the attempts taken to thread a bead, jump through a hoop or ask peers for support. There are observations that happen through looking around or participant observation that allows the observer to record at intervals whenever possible and at other times teach the class. Alternatively, there may be a diary entry each day at a certain time, although there is the difficulty of each day being different and there may be disruption to the schedule on a particular day. With these methods, it is wise to be selective in the information you gather because it is impossible to record everything that happens, even in a short space of time. Teaching is so multifaceted that whilst you are noticing one thing, another may be occurring elsewhere that is not recorded. It is therefore important, if you want specific information, to plan the observation in detail and be prepared to abandon it if circumstances dictate that this is not an appropriate time. Many things can affect the observation taking place, such as a windy, snowy or hot day or an impending Ofsted inspection.

Whatever the approach, it is important to first decide what you want to observe, how you will record it and what you will do with the information when you have obtained it. For example, you may need to decide for how long you will observe, at what time in the day and on what day of the week, as all of these may affect the data gathered. You need to decide whether you will observe the pupil in an isolated situation or in a group interaction, and when the data is gathered you need to decide which of it is significant, for example, whether it usefully indicates that learning has taken place, that there has been social development or that the pupil has mastered a new skill and ways forward for future learning.

Additionally, there are planned and unplanned observations. Clearly, if you purposefully set out to gather qualitative or quantitative observational data, then this needs careful planning, organising and orchestrating. However, anecdotal observations are also an assessment technique that is more commonly used in early years education. Often, Post-its or tick charts will be available for early years practitioners to quickly note down the learning witnessed that will later be added to the pupil's profile data, but this perhaps is much less frequently used with older pupils in primary school.

Observation techniques aid in assessing difficult situations such as deciphering whether a pupil is thinking or daydreaming; concentrating or doodling (Wragg, 2001). Informal observation is a key skill of a teacher, such as being able to know who needs support, who has lost interest, which groups work well together, whether the pupils are using the resources effectively and who has completed the task, but this is a monitoring exercise, noticing the ordinary happenings, rather than a more formal observation. It is no less important than more formal observation techniques and can offer rich data if it can be processed and important details emerge from the whole situation being observed. Being an expert in focused, formal observations heightens the ability to notice key learning points incidentally (Edgington, 2004). It is a valuable technique because it offers a more rounded assessment of pupils' learning than a test paper can offer; a test very often assesses the reading or writing ability of the pupil rather than evaluating the particular learning taking place in the subject – for example, science or history.

More formal observations create ethical dilemmas, as if pupils know they are being observed they may change their behaviour. If they are not told, would this be ethical? Although you may sit on a low chair away from the action, keep a low profile and be as inconspicuous as possible when observing, how will you react when a pupil asks you a question or asks you for help? Similarly, even though you aim for neutrality, it may be difficult to divorce your own feelings, opinions and views from what you are observing. For example, you observe a pupil in the playground who in earlier years has been thought to have started many altercations. It may be possible to construe a genuine conversation with an unlikely fellow pupil as threatening behaviour if you are not within earshot of what is being said. Similarly, if you have had children yourself or have close relatives with young children, then you may be influenced by your own or your family and friends' views of child development and learning when observing pupils in primary school. Perhaps the most important point of using observations in primary school is to be holistic, acknowledging pupils' learning, social and emotional development and life experiences so that the data gathered can support and enhance the future learning of the pupils in your class. The development of primary-aged children is complex but fascinating and observation offers an insight into pupils' worlds and how they learn best.

It may be appropriate to use audio or video recordings which provide a complete record of what was said and the actions that took place rather than having a written record, provided it does not interfere with normal classroom practices. Photographs are also being used much more frequently in primary schools to evidence learning.

In one way, observing pupils' learning could be thought of as a luxury, as taking time out of the normal classroom routine to note what is happening, how pupils are learning and how they interact with their peers. It may also require a shift in teaching and learning styles for observation to be part of daily or weekly routines. It is your choice whether you adopt observation as an assessment technique but it may be helpful to observe how experienced early years teachers weave observation into their daily practice.

Mind maps and concept maps

Mind maps and, perhaps to a lesser extent, concept maps are being increasingly used as an assessment strategy in primary school. The word 'mapping' itself means the use of a pictorial strategy to arrange key themes and concepts and is used in business and social sciences as a learning or discussion strategy. This section will discuss how both mind maps and concept maps can be used to assess primary pupils. A variety of teaching strategies use 'mapping' such as story mapping which, not surprisingly, is the plan of a story. This section, though, is concerned purely with mind maps and concept maps and their wider focus which is applicable across the curriculum. Mind maps and concept maps are thought to be the paper version of technological organisers. There are computer packages that specifically use mind maps, such as Mind Genius, Edraw or Mind Meister, which can perform the same function as a mind map by classifying data. The advantage of using mind maps electronically is that use can be made of hyperlinks and other digital or technological information to enhance the information placed on the map. Both mind maps and concept maps can be used as personal learning or revision tools by pupils or you as the teacher.

Mind maps

Mind maps are creative and focus on visual representations working on both the imagination and the association of facts. They were developed by Tony Buzan (2004) following his research on the psychology of learning, thinking and remembering. Mind map plans use pictures with text, several concepts being connected on one page. They are extremely versatile in that they can be applied to almost any situation in most professions from project management to chiropractice. Mind maps are a visual representation of words, ideas and thoughts that are symbolised in a diagram or map. Buzan and Buzan (2003) suggest that by working from the centre outwards, mind maps have three principles: emphasis, association and clarity. Emphasis requires using a central word, phrase or picture, using images throughout, variations in size of font, at least three different colours and organisation of the branches, pictures and words. Association necessitates using arrows for connection, colours and codes. Clarity entails using only one key word, connecting all branches to the central image and keeping your mind map as clear as possible, printing the words and drawing clearly defined branches. Mind maps encourage the mind to follow the same path, working from a central idea to peripheral connections.

Mind maps provide a multisensory opportunity to integrate and merge ideas and are thought to aid pupils in retaining knowledge and skills, and enhance comprehension, extend learning potential and increase motivation (Karge, 2006). They can engage both parts of the brain as they involve both creative and logical thought processes and respond to a diverse range of learning styles. Buzan (2004) continues to explain that lists and sequences involve left-brain activity but to be creative you need to activate your right brain as well, which can interpret colour, images and spatial awareness. Using both sides of the brain allows each side to link with the other, creating stronger links and leading to increased creativity. Using mind maps, therefore, should enable pupils to engage in heightened learning and allow you to assess this potential.

Mind maps can generate and record a large amount of data and illustrate the relationships between different ideas that increase mental agility (Mento et al., 1999). They approach the information in a holistic way with personal experiences, skills and prior knowledge and understanding used to form the connections that aid profound and deep learning through visual organisation and integration with a range of cognitive brain functions that are needed for learning (Nast, 2006).

Their flexibility is perhaps their main advantage as they can be used for anything from exploring an initial idea to planning your career or your life (Buzan, 2004). They can be used for personal note taking or revision and as an interactive teaching, learning and assessment strategy in the classroom. The advantages of using mind maps for your class and yourself are that they can help solve problems through planning and organisation, develop creativity, clarify situations and offer different perspectives on a situation which can save you time and generate a feeling of intellectual creativity in which pupils (and you) are less stressed and can enjoy working more fully. They are also a simple way in which you can assess the learning of pupils.

Constructing a mind map is simple and can be used throughout primary school. It involves writing a key theme in the centre of an A3-sized piece of plain paper. A3 plain paper is used as it is thought to encourage creativity, free from the constraints of lined or A4 paper which may limit the number of branches used. From the central theme, the pupil would draw branches using coloured pens or crayons and write key words in relevant places. Sub-branches may then be created which may be of different length and importance but would also have coloured pictures and words attached to them. As the sub-branches appear, it may be that some connect through a similar knowledge, thought, action or skill which may be represented by a different colour.

It is thought that if pictures and words are seen simultaneously this facilitates the links between short- and long-term memory (Rega, 1993), leading to deeper learning and enhanced recall of facts (Farrand et al., 2002). Farrand et al. (2002) also found that motivation levels were higher and there was heightened critical thinking when mind maps were used.

This is a technique that requires practice by pupils if the full benefits of mind maps are to be gained. They can be used at various times of the lesson or unit of work, encouraging pupils to be actively involved in monitoring and assessing their own learning. Mind maps can be used at different times of the day, lesson or unit of work. At the beginning, they may be used for gathering knowledge on prior learning. For example, with the word 'electricity' in the centre pupils could draw branches that represent all they know about electricity. If this mind map is kept, then part way through the unit of work on electricity, pupils could add further things they now know in a different colour which highlights their learning. Similarly, this process may be used at the end of the unit on electricity where pupils, again using a different colour, add the new knowledge they have gained since the mid-point. Pupils may then share with another pupil or the rest of the class and pupils could then update their mind maps with the extra knowledge gained from other pupils. The finished mind map proves a useful aid for revision and allows you to accurately record each pupil's learning. Using mind maps provides a positive opportunity for you to assess pupils and they will not feel as though they are being tested.

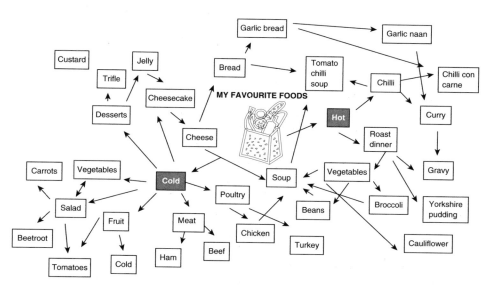

Figure 7.1   An example of a mind map (the shaded boxes represent the start of the mind map)

Concept maps

Concept maps are another organisational technique, different from a mind map in that concept maps are represented hierarchically (Eppler, 2006). A concept map illustrates the systematic relationship between the main and sub-theories or hypotheses and needs to be read from top to bottom (Hay and Kinchin, 2006). They can be used for self-study and revision as well as for a teaching, learning and assessment strategy in classroom teaching.

They are fundamentally different to mind maps in that they are ranked in order of importance, are linear and contain no colour or pictures. The central theory or concept is placed at the top of the page and sub-themes or subordinate concepts are written below. They could be placed within the context of the overall learning style and multiple intelligence theories. It can also be known as *clustering* and can be used as a brainstorming activity. There are three simple rules that govern concept maps (Novak, 1984): first, the key word or point of the concept map is placed at the top of a page with less important facts or links placed elsewhere; second, the 'concepts' are linked with lines and explanatory words or sentences; and third, there may be numerous links although the 'concepts' must only be listed once. It is perhaps a more demanding strategy than mind maps but the concept route map created offers an opportunity for a robust form of assessment through a clear illustration of the learning, of misconceptions and of surface or deep learning. From there, of course, it will highlight the sections that need to be revised through homework or further teaching.

It is the structure of the concept map that is the key to a robust assessment possibility. Research (Westbrook, 1998) indicates that concept maps can enhance learning if used as an assessment strategy. Concept maps may be used with two or more pupils in collaboration working on a single concept map. This enables pupils to share knowledge and skills and develop social skills (Wandersee, 1990). Joint concept maps, though, may pose more of a problem when assessing the learning of individual pupils, as it may not be clear who is responsible for which part of the concept map.

Finally, concept maps, as mind maps, can be used as assessment strategies detailing what pupils know, understand or can do. They can also be used in subjects such as science or maths, illustrating the thinking process by which an experiment or computation has been undertaken. The effectiveness of both mind maps and concept maps is in the organisation of thoughts, ideas and knowledge. As a teacher, you may also use

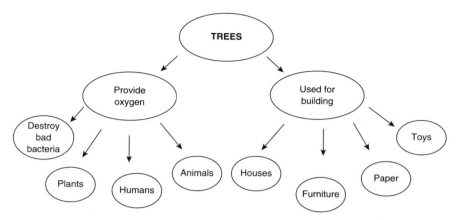

Figure 7.2   An example of a concept map (layers can be added at the bottom)

these techniques to organise your teaching and resources or to arrange your daily and weekly schedules in order of importance.

 Points for Reflection

- Observation techniques are a common strategy for teachers to assess pupils' learning in the classroom.
- The ethical implications of observations need consideration.
- Observation techniques can be used throughout primary school.
- There must be caution in making judgements based on limited evidence that may be biased.
- It is worth taking time to think about how you could use mind maps or concept maps for assessment purposes in your class.
- Both getting the most out of observations and developing mind and concept maps as assessment strategies will take time for you and the pupils to perfect.

 Further Reading

Bauman, J.F. and Bergeron, B. (1993) 'Story Map Instructions Using Children's Literature: Effects on First Graders' Comprehension of Central Narrative Elements', *Journal of Literacy Research*, 25, p. 407.

(Continued)

(Continued)

Budd, J.W. (2004) 'Mind Maps as Classroom Exercises', *The Journal of Economic Education*, 35(1): 35–46.

Buzan, T. and Buzan, B. (2000) *The Mind Map Book*. London: BBC Worldwide.

Hamm, M. and Adams, D. (2009) *Activating Assessment for all Students*. Lanham, MD: Rowman & Littlefield.

Harlen, W. (2007) *Assessment of Learning*. London: SAGE.

Jitlakoat, Y. (2005) 'The Effectiveness of Using Concept Mapping to Improve Primary Medical Care Nursing Competencies among Fourth Year Assumption University Nursing Students', Assumption University, Bangkok, Thailand, 9(2): 111–20.

Lambert, D. and Lines, D. (2000) *Understanding Assessment: Purposes, Perceptions, Practice*. London: RoutledgeFalmer.

Montgomery, D. (1999) *Positive Teacher Appraisal through Classroom Observation*. London: David Fulton.

CHAPTER 8

USING QUESTIONING, EXPLAINING, CIRCLE TIME AND DEBATES

Chapter Objectives

1 To understand different strategies to assess pupils
2 To understand that assessment can promote speaking and listening
3 To know how to use questioning, explaining, circle time and debates to assess pupils' learning

---

Questioning

Questioning is one of the most common forms of classroom assessment and one with which you will be most familiar. You will probably recognise that questioning is an integral part of your professional practice. It is a teaching and assessment strategy that should challenge pupils and can also maintain the pace and interest of your lesson. Through differentiated questions, you can encourage pupils to think and explain, adapt the situation and become more confident orators. Questions can be asked to individuals or small groups or be addressed to the whole class; it is important to plan the questions carefully so that they are appropriate for the pupils you teach and challenge and develop their thinking skills.

Research (Clarke, 2001) suggests that many of the questions teachers ask are closed questions that are unproductive, whereas open questions can make increased cognitive demands on the pupil, requiring them to think beyond the literal. We will look at these two types in further detail later on in this chapter. Wragg (2001) also suggests that most teachers' questions relate to checking knowledge and understanding of the subject matter, not to the process of thinking. Further research, also by Clarke (2001), found that teachers only wait two seconds before answering a question themselves, whereas the ideal waiting time would be at least five seconds to allow pupils to process the question and search for an answer.

There are different ways in which you can wait for a minimum of five seconds before answering your own question. One idea might be to use a technique called *think-pair-share*. This requires pupils to think of the answer, then share with a fellow pupil and finally share with the class, as explained earlier in this book. Similarly, snowballing is a strategy you can use to engage pupils in dialogue. Each pupil needs a piece of paper plus a writing implement. They write the answer on the paper, then screw up the paper. On your instruction, they throw the 'snowball' somewhere in the room. Each pupil then gathers up one snowball and reads out the answer. They can then agree or disagree but if you ask them for the answer on the paper, the responsibility of getting it right is lightened as it is not their own answer. It also relieves the fact that quick thinkers will always put up their hands first, which may lead to slower thinkers switching off as they do not feel involved. Additionally, the teacher may use a clicker which is a handheld device with which pupils can respond to your questions. The results can be displayed on a whiteboard and again there is anonymity to the answers pupils give.

Teachers' reasons for asking questions differ from those we use in conversations outside the classroom, in that within the classroom the aim is to ascertain what pupils know, whereas outside the classroom teachers often ask questions to find out something for themselves. You may ask questions in your classroom to engender curiosity, to focus attention, to structure a task or to provide an opportunity for pupils to assimilate the learning and reflect upon it. You may also ask 'secretarial' questions such as 'Where is your book?' or 'Whose turn is it to take the register?' Reasons for asking questions therefore can vary between the cognitive (knowledge and understanding), affective (emotional), social and procedural. The specific questioning that this chapter is about involves questioning as an assessment tool.

It is important that questions are framed carefully to ensure the information gained is useful and that you consider whether there may be an alternative way to attain the information, such as by using a mind map, as discussed in the previous chapter. Questions can be categorised into two types: lower order, such as those relating to facts, management, organisation and timetabling; and higher order, which require reasoning, application of knowledge and synthesis of ideas. These questions may also be known as closed and open questions such as: 'Who did Little Red Riding Hood visit?' or 'What would happen if Red Riding Hood had arrived at her grandmother's house before the wolf?'

Closed questions are quite limited in the response that can be offered whilst open questions offer a choice of answers that may be given. Closed questioning as an assessment strategy limits the information you can gain as it usually involves a mere recall of facts relating to the curriculum subject under review. Open questions, however, offer an opportunity for the pupil to demonstrate strategic thinking. For example, in maths you could ask: 'What is the sum of 34 and 62?' This would, hopefully, result in an answer of 96. However, should you ask, 'How many different ways can you get to the number 96?', you would allow pupils to demonstrate a range of computational strategies, thereby indicating an understanding that there are different ways of arriving at the number 96. Similarly, topics may begin with questions to assess pupils' learning such as: 'Where do the puddles go when the sun is out?' or 'Why does my shadow grow longer and shorter and sometimes disappear altogether?' The most effective questions are those in which there may be more than one answer. This also takes the pressure off pupils thinking there is only one answer to the question or that you are only looking for a particular answer which results in an episode of 'guess what is in the teacher's head' syndrome.

Bloom's taxonomy (Bloom and Krathwohl, 1956) explains how questions at different levels can increasingly challenge the thinking of pupils. Bloom's principle was that a question is not worth asking if it does not generate thinking; alternatively, this could be thought of as: questions are only as good as the answers they get. Bloom and Krathwohl (1956) categorised questions into six main groups: knowledge, comprehension, application, analysis, synthesis and evaluation. Ideas for questions that could be asked in each of these categories are given in Figure 8.1.

Knowledge	What happened after . . .?
	How many . . .?
	Who was it that . . .?
	Can you name the . . .?
	Describe what happened at . . .
	Who spoke to . . .?
	What is the meaning of . . .?
	What is . . .?
	Which is true or false . . .?
Comprehension	Can you write in your own words . . .?
	Can you write a brief outline . . .?
	What do you think might happen next . . .?
	Who do you think . . .?
	What was the main idea . . .?
	Who was the key character . . .?
	Can you distinguish between . . .?
	What differences exist between . . .?
	Can you provide an example of what you mean . . .?
	Can you provide a definition for . . .?
Application	Can you think of another instance where . . .?
	Could this have happened in . . .?
	Can you group by characteristics such as . . .?
	What factors would you change if . . .?
	Can you apply the method used to some experience of your own . . .?
	What questions would you ask of . . .?
	From the information given, can you develop a set of instructions about . . .?
	Would this information be useful if you had a . . .?
Analysis	Which events could have happened . . .?
	If . . . happened, what might the ending have been?
	How was this similar to . . .?
	What was the underlying theme of . . .?
	What do you see as other possible outcomes?
	Why did . . . changes occur?
	Can you compare your . . . with that presented in . . .?
	Can you explain what must have happened when . . .?
	How is . . . similar to . . .?
	What are some of the problems of . . .?
	Can you distinguish between . . .?
	What were some of the motives behind . . .?
	What was the turning point in the game . . .?
	What was the problem with . . .?

Synthesis	Can you design a . . . to . . .?
	Why not compose a song about . . .?
	Can you see a possible solution to . . .?
	If you had access to all resources how would you deal with . . .?
	Why don't you devise your own way to deal with . . .?
	What would happen if . . .?
	How many ways can you . . .?
	Can you create new and unusual uses for . . .?
	Can you write a new recipe for a tasty dish?
	Can you develop a proposal which would . . .?
Evaluation	Is there a better solution to?
	Judge the value of...
	Defend your position...
	Do you think ...?
	How would you have ...?
	What changes would you recommend? Why?
	How would you feel if ...?
	How effective is ...?
	What do you think about? Why?

Figure 8.1 Bloom's taxonomy questions

You will notice that there are key words in each of these sections, from knowledge-based questions to those that require some form of evaluation:

Knowledge: Who? What? When? Where? Find. Show. Name. How many? Which?

Comprehension: Can you...? What was...? What do you think? Compare, explain, classify.

Application: Could/would/can you? Apply, use, experiment, organise.

Analysis: How, if, examine, simplify, classify, dissect.

Synthesis: Why don't you? How many...? Build, construct, imagine, propose.

Evaluation: How effective? Judge, defend, justify, prove, disprove, explain, compare.

Wragg and Brown (2001) suggest three other ways in which questions may be categorised: first, *conceptual* questions, for example sorting materials by different properties. With these questions, you may use Bloom and Krathwohl-type questions to draw out the reasons for pupils' actions. Second, *empirical* questions involve observation and recall of information with reasoning only being used to confirm factual knowledge. Finally, *value* questions are those concerned with the emotions, morals and health issues such as global warming, smoking or genetically modified food.

In order for you to ask effective questions, it is a good idea to plan and structure them, providing signposts along pupils' learning journeys. There may be questions to stimulate interest in a topic followed by questions to ascertain prior learning, questions to enable thinking about the learning of a particular lesson, and finally questions to check what learning has taken place. Wragg and Brown (2001) suggest that key tactics for effective questioning, along with structuring, are: pitching questions at the right level, taking note of Bloom and Krathwohl's taxonomy (1956), directing questions to specific pupils or a group of pupils, pausing for reflection and pacing the lesson so that it is interesting and stimulating, prompting answers and probing deeper into other answers, and listening and responding appropriately so that pupils are furthered in their learning through your assessment of their present knowledge and understanding.

Questions may be asked at the start, in the middle or at the end of a lesson or a topic to ascertain prior or learnt knowledge, skills or understanding, but, as is evident in the rest of this chapter, in the previous chapter and in the following two chapters, there are other ways in which this information may be gained.

Explaining

Teachers' explanations can have immense impact on pupils' learning. The words 'explain' and 'explanation' can be used in different contexts, such as a prelude to a reprimand, to clarify understanding or to explain cause and effect. However the words are used, explaining involves passing on understanding to another person. This section of the chapter is not concerned with you explaining concepts to pupils, but instead with pupils explaining to you so that you can assess their knowledge, skills or understanding. It is perhaps the least used strategy in primary school but allows pupils to explain something to you, to a peer or to a group of peers and can be used effectively as an assessment strategy.

Pupils may need to practise or need support in offering explanations and it may fall to you to structure the explanation so that it is presented in a succinct, clear and logical manner or to offer the language needed to fulfil the task. Through pupils' explanations, you will be able to identify any misunderstanding or misconceptions that may arise and either allow other pupils to interject to correct these or make a note to cover these in future lessons. It is possible to ask pupils to explain to you a range of learning such as understanding, concepts, procedures, purposes, knowledge, processes and consequences, and to effectively use their voices and gestures and appropriate resources to support their explanation.

Asking pupils to provide explanations can be spontaneous or planned. For example, if a group has clearly understood how to construct a compound sentence but another group has not, then this may be an opportunity for those who understand to explain to the others their understanding of this concept. Alternatively, you may ask a group of pupils to prepare an explanation to the class on the way in which the group worked together using their knowledge of structures to build a chair that would support a half-litre bottle of water. Explanations by pupils can serve three purposes. First, they consolidate the learning of the pupil presenters; second, they provide information for other pupils who can compare and improve their knowledge and understanding by listening to their peers; and third, they give you a clear indication of their learning and application of this knowledge. Additionally, they encourage pupils to become more autonomous learners and develop the cross-curricular link of enhancing different strategies in speaking and listening.

When teaching pupils strategies for explanations, it may be useful to consult Wragg and Brown's (2001: 56) features of good explanation. These use a clear structure, planning what to say, and using clear and uncomplicated language, although this can include specific terminology connected with the topic, using a clear voice which is varied in pitch, has good pace and is supported by body gestures, fluency including enthusiasm which generates interest and using a range of strategies such as examples, analogies, practical examples or teaching aids.

Another effective way of assessing pupils is through circle time and although this may be thought of as a strategy to use with younger pupils, it can be very effective with older pupils in primary school, as seen by the Social and Emotional Aspects of Learning (SEAL) strategy (DfES, 2005) which promotes circle time across all key stages in primary school. The SEAL (DfES, 2005) strategy, although not current government policy, provides a wealth of activities for pupils throughout primary schooling to develop the social and emotional aspects of learning, thereby enabling pupils to control their behaviour in order that learning can be enhanced.

Circle time

The social and emotional aspects of learning are important as they are the tools with which pupils gain confidence and grow in self-esteem and self-efficacy. Pupils may not be able to provide explanations to their peers, as described in the section above, without being socially and emotionally secure in their knowledge and understanding. Therefore, circle time has the ability to motivate through discussion in a safe environment. It also offers an opportunity for you to assess the social and emotional well-being of pupils, which in turn affects their enthusiasm and incentive to learn.

Each circle time session has a five-stage structure. The first two stages set the scene and the parameters; the middle section explores the theme; and the final two sections work to a close where all pupils leave feeling calm and positive. Circle time can involve teaching, discussing, thinking and problem solving and should ideally move at a brisk pace, and can also be used as a cross-curricular tool. All sessions involve concentrating, looking, listening, speaking and thinking (Mosley, 2006). This section concentrates on circle time as an assessment tool for evaluating the social and emotional well-being of pupils.

Like anything in teaching, unless you are well prepared for circle time it may not progress as well as you would like. Even if you have planned it well, it may take a turn that you had not predicted and you may need to decide whether to maintain your original plan or go with the flow of the topic of conversation. It is also important to establish three main ground rules so that all pupils understand that: everyone has a right to say what they want; everyone has a right to stay silent and not offer an opinion; and everyone is kind and positive to others.

Circle time can be used effectively to explore issues raised in the classroom or playground such as disagreement, unkindness or anger. Through allowing pupils to offer their thought processes, it will be possible for you to tap into their learning processes. Pupils learn in different ways and approach assessment with different feelings. Exploring feelings can offer you insight into how each pupil 'ticks'. This information is not thought of as a test but you will be assessing their readiness for learning and can use this to your advantage when preparing lessons and future assessments in other subjects.

Relationships can be explored through a wide range of strategies such as stories, toys, video extracts and puppets. Circle time can be used to explore changes either to the class as a whole or to individuals who may be facing changes within their home life, and it can also be used as a vehicle to explore aspirations and achievement of goals. For younger pupils, it may be useful to use puppets or other toys to explore issues such as friendship, bullying and kindness. If the puppets act out a scene, then pupils can be encouraged to offer opinions on what should be said or done in order to improve the situation. It offers imagery so that pupils do not need to refer to particular people or pupils when exploring their feelings. Similarly, stories – particularly fairy stories – can be a catalyst for the discussion of sensitive topics. For example, was Goldilocks right to go inside the bears' house? Was Red Riding Hood safe to walk through the forest to her grandmother's? Why did Sleeping Beauty eat the apple when she was told not to? Have you thought about the story of the three little pigs from the wolf's perspective? There are many examples of stories that explore difficult issues and for each session you will assess the general feeling of pupils, plus note anything out of the ordinary such as someone getting very upset or agitated, which may need to be explored in more depth without singling out the pupil in question.

Whatever the subject of your circle time, the purpose is to assess the social and emotional status of the pupils you teach and to build strong, resilient pupils who are confident in attaining their goals and aspirations through encouragement, praise and an understanding of the impact of certain behaviours on other pupils. It is important to remember also that circle time offers you an opportunity to assess pupils in a different way from the normal classroom situation and may highlight to you why certain pupils react in certain ways to different things. This will aid your planning and teaching strategies, which should in turn allow pupils to feel happy and motivated to learn.

Debates

There is little research and guidance on developing debates with primary-aged pupils but in many respects it is just another way of asking questions and pupils explaining. As a change from asking questions, you can make a statement and ask pupils to discuss it in pairs or groups, or you can divide the class into larger groups and ask them to prepare their case to debate a certain issue. For example:

- Why did Henry VIII have six wives? Discuss.
- People should be fined if they do not recycle all their waste. Discuss.
- How would life be different if the Victorians had had mobile phones? Discuss.
- Should Heathrow build a new runway? Divide into two groups and argue for and against.
- Should pupils be allowed to decide what they wear in school? Divide into two groups and argue for and against.
- Should pupils be able to use text language in tests? Divide into two groups and argue for and against.

In a similar but more diversified way, you may choose to use De Bono's Six Thinking Hats (1995) to encourage pupils to argue different points of view. This technique encourages dialogue and develops speaking, listening and decision making. There are six 'hats' which may be represented as hats or as coloured chairs, paper, plastic cups or whatever can be gathered in the colours of red, white, black, yellow, green and blue. Each hat represents a different emotion and pupils need to argue the case in hand from that viewpoint. The red hat represents intuitive or instinctive gut reactions or statements of emotional feeling (but necessarily with justification); the white hat represents neutral feelings that are objective and informative; the black is the analyst who provides a logical and systematic but negative argument; the yellow represents optimism and positivity, seeing the best side of things; the green hat is creative, offering ideas and possibilities; and the blue hat is the cool group who are organised, work to an agenda, work through processes, have an overview of the whole situation and can easily form a decision. Using this method will allow pupils to engage in communication and debate without any risk, as the 'hat' takes away personal responsibility. It also allows them to realise that there are different opinions or perspectives on every issue and encourages creative thinking in different and multiple ways. The six hats should present in a logical order with the white group beginning, presenting the facts, and the green following, offering ideas on ways forward. Next would be the yellow group who would state the positives and benefits of the project or issue being debated, followed by the black group who would point out the drawbacks. The red group would then ask for thoughts and feelings about the choices offered after considering the benefits and drawbacks, and finally the blue group would summarise the situation and offer ways in which to move forward. This can also be tried with very young pupils who can merely offer their ideas, the advantages and disadvantages and decide on a way forward. For example, should they play out in the snow? Do they need to put on their coat for playtime? With older pupils, you may debate healthy food, the environment, a topic in the news or issues that develop from books or the National Curriculum, such as a character change in a story or the ethics of the Ancient Egyptians weighing the heart to ascertain the purity of the deceased person.

In many ways, during any debate or discussion, you observe the pupils and listen in order to assess their knowledge and understanding of a subject or, in literacy, their skills in speaking and listening. In a rapidly developing world, it is vital that children develop the skills of thinking, reasoning, collaboration and problem solving.

To conclude, this chapter has offered a range of assessment strategies that also develop pupils' speaking and listening skills, and give them an understanding of their feelings and an opportunity to take control of their own learning.

 Points for Reflection

1 Think about the type and purpose of the questions you ask.
2 Change the focus of your lessons so that pupils are illustrating what they can do rather than you leading the session with your questions.
3 Think about how you deploy the strategies in this chapter in order to develop and extend pupils' speaking and listening skills as well.
4 Choose different ways in which pupils can respond such as think-pair-share, voting and snowballing.
5 Wait at least five seconds for a pupil's response.

 Further Reading

Black, P., Harrison, C., Lee, C., Marshall, B. and Wiliam, D. (2003) *Assessment for Learning: Putting it into Practice*. Maidenhead: Open University Press.

Collins, M. (2007) *Circle Time for the Very Young*. London: Paul Chapman.

Davies, I. (2011) *Debates in History Teaching*. Abingdon: Routledge.

Hayes, D. (2006) *Inspiring Primary Teaching: Insights into Excellent Primary Practice*. Exeter: Learning Matters.

Hayes, D. (2007) *Joyful Teaching and Learning in the Primary School*. Exeter: Learning Matters.

Hughes, P. (2008) *Principles of Primary Education*, 3rd edition. London: David Fulton.

Simon, K.G. (2001) *Moral Questions in the Classroom: How to Get Kids to Think Deeply about Real Life and their School Work*. New York: R.R. Donnelly & Sons.

Vickery, A. (2013) *Developing Active Learning in the Primary Classroom*. London: SAGE.

Wragg, E.C. (2001) *Explaining in the Primary School*. London: Routledge.

CHAPTER 9

REPORTS, ROLE PLAY, POSTERS, LEARNING JOURNALS AND PORTFOLIOS

Chapter Objectives

1. To understand that there are different ways in which to assess pupils
2. To understand that assessments need to be planned
3. To understand that pupils learn in many different ways and different places that can be explored through role play
4. To understand that pupils have ownership of their own learning
5. To understand that the organisation of the classroom and the shift of balance between teacher and pupil can enhance learning

Role play

Role play can take many forms but the basic fact is that you are asking pupils to imagine either they are themselves in a different time or space or they are someone else in a particular situation. Pupils can be real people, imaginary people or themselves, and situations can be recognisable or unknown, normal or extraordinary. Using role play, pupils may learn about new situations, how to deal with awkward circumstances, gain an understanding of or empathy with a character or learn new facts or skills. Through social-dramatic and thematic role play, pupils are encouraged to act out imaginary and real-life situations and to develop imaginative and social skills that will help them make connections with their learning. Role-play situations can help pupils make sense of the world, build concepts and skills, control behaviour, take risks, experiment with language and think creatively. Young children naturally create imagined situations and characters and role play is an extension of this.

The word 'role' comes from the roll of parchment on which an actor's part was written and therefore originates from dramatic use (Van Ments, 1983). Throughout our daily life, we find ourselves acting out various situations – when out shopping, going to the dentist, going on holiday – and Joyce Grenfell (1910–1979) singer, commedienne, and actor, famous for her monologues once described teaching as 80 per cent role play and 20 per cent teaching. If you stop to think of the many different roles you take on during the course of a week of teaching, it would be endless. It may possibly include: nose wiper, social worker, arbitrator, government directive reader, surrogate parent, encyclopaedia or public relations officer. Consequently, it seems as though, as adults, we are all experts at role play as it is vital to life in modern society.

However, there is a specific difference between role play and acting. Acting is bringing to life a character in order to entertain an audience. Role play is concerned with people trying to feel, react and conduct themselves in the way that another person, real or imagined, would behave in a particular situation. Role play has a simple structure of the parameters of the situation and the role players. It can last for a few minutes to 30 or 40 minutes or even longer if required. Following a role play, it is good for you to explore the issues raised during the session. Role play can be a powerful enabling tool in a teacher's repertoire as it offers an opportunity to place pupils in situations they would not usually encounter in their lives, where they can explore sensitive or emotional issues. Role play can therefore be used as a teaching or assessment strategy for developing knowledge, skills or understanding. It is a much more powerful tool than reading or being told information and involves deep learning. Similarly, it offers a safe position from which to explore a range of issues if pupils are not playing themselves or they are exploring a situation out of their experience. Role play is often used for exploring feelings, problems or behaviours or used as a teaching tool across all National Curriculum subjects. It is an inclusive teaching and assessment strategy as it offers an opportunity for those less able at writing to excel and is an active activity that can provide immediate assessment opportunities and feedback.

Although role play is not a difficult concept, there are potential disadvantages and the remedy for most of these rests with you as teacher. For example, it is important not to over-simplify the situation or allow the proceedings to become flippant or trivial, and you must always keep tight control of the time and resources used. At best, pupils will leave after an enjoyable and exciting experience with a greater understanding of the situation explored. At worst however, pupils may be embarrassed, bored and disinterested, not understanding how the experience fits into their learning. In this case, they will take little knowledge or understanding away from the experience.

Early years departments use role play naturally as part of their daily routines. There is often a role-play area where pupils can become a range of people such as a shop assistant, a check-in operator at an airport, a character in the Nativity or a construction worker. Pupils in early Key Stage 2 may also have role-play areas set up in or just outside their classroom which may involve, for example, supporting and practising a modern foreign language or transforming themselves into an ancient Egyptian. However, role-play areas in upper Key Stage 2 are perhaps less popular. This may be because other adults such as parents and governors see role play as playing not learning. There are two points to address here. If role play is conducted appropriately, much learning and assessment can take place. Second, even if it were just play, this is still a powerful strategy for learning provided it is structured and overseen by you as the teacher.

Role play for the purpose of assessment needs to be planned. Whereas early years practitioners are skilled at providing structured role-play situations and know clearly what they are assessing, this may not be a skill that is practised or readily used throughout the rest of primary school. However, schools might invite a drama group into school to 'transport' pupils back to Victorian times, for example. Pupils are invited to take part in this 'drama' and learn much from handling artefacts and observing the different way life was in historical times. Similarly, visits to places that can recreate the Tudor times or a Second World War setting, so that pupils can experience the sounds and smells of that time, provide powerful learning opportunities that cannot be replicated through books, internet searches or digital means. In these situations, other adults lead the role play and the pupils join in. There are also situations where pupils can take on the full role themselves, such as hot seating.

For hot seating, pupils need to have some prior knowledge of the situation or person they are playing. One such scenario could be for you to choose a group to be Henry VIII and several of his courtiers.

The rest of the class interview them on various aspects of Henry VIII's life to gain a fuller picture of what life was like at this time. For example, pupils may ask why Henry VIII beheaded Anne Boleyn, ask a servant what his life was like, ask Katherine Parr what she felt like when Henry VIII died, ask what clothes they wore, what hobbies they had or what food they ate. It may be that the groups in the class have each been asked to research a particular aspect of Tudor life and each group takes turns at being in the hot seat. Similarly, this strategy can explore contemporary issues, for example around a planned project to demolish a local playground and park and replace it with a supermarket. Through use of hot seating, pupils can develop knowledge of others' opinions, understand that there are always at least two sides to every issue and develop persuasive language which can then be transferred into their writing in this genre. With younger pupils, hot seating can be used, for example, in geography following pupils' return from holiday. Pupils can find out about different places, languages, foods, climates and clothes. In science Key Stage 2, you may lead the class in a role-play activity to explain the water cycle, magnetism or the planets in order from the sun; in maths for younger pupils, role play can illustrate simple calculations; in literacy, pupils of any age can use role play to re-enact their stories for which an ending still needs to be written. Exploring different endings of a story through role play can offer alternative options to those originally thought of. It can explore different perceptions, ideas and concepts and is a useful teaching strategy for inclusion, motivation and learning.

Assessment of role play in its simplest terms is in observing the situation. However, assessment will be much easier and more useful if there are clear learning objectives and you know exactly what and which pupils you are assessing. In addition to role play being a powerful learning strategy, it offers a significant opportunity to observe and assess what pupils have learnt, whether this be focused on knowledge, skills or understanding or the emotional and social skills developed.

Displays and posters

You may know the National Curriculum well and be aware of the need to stimulate and motivate pupils in order for them to be excited to learn. However, although you know that displays should be interesting, stimulating and interactive, you may not have had an opportunity to plan and create many different displays yourself. Interactive displays engage pupils physically and cognitively and can challenge them to solve problems, investigate, follow instructions, develop opinions and imaginative ideas and record their learning.

Creating a display that has impact on pupils' learning needs to be planned carefully and systematically. Consideration should be given to the focus of the learning, the intention of the display, how pupils will benefit from it and how they can gain access to it. You need to first consider the colours you will use, and if you want to know which colours complement each other you can find this out through an internet search for 'colour wheels'. Usually, you need bright, vivid colours rather than neutral (beige or white) shades which will attract interest in and engagement with the display. If you want to include artefacts, articles or objects in your display, you may like to visit a car boot sale or charity shop. Once you have all your materials, you need to decide how to mount your objects, words and photographs. It is also a good idea to use a border and double-back your display items; you may also like to vary shape and size. Although this takes time, it is the basis of a quality display (Andrew-Power and Gormley, 2009). It is important that pupils can see and read the display; words or sentences are best seen if font size 72 is used. Displays can be created in any and all National Curriculum subjects and in many different spaces, including hanging information on a 'washing line'. In order to use display as a learning strategy rather than as a passive account of pupils' work, pupils need to be able to interact with the display such as lifting flaps, spinning wheels, adding words, sentences and numbers, and as such hook and loop fasteners like Velcro (de Mestral patent, 1955) are a useful tool for interactive displays.

Other ways in which display can be used effectively in the classroom are: instead of a worksheet requiring pupils to place numbers in a grid reference; to add their own 'powerful words' on the literacy display; as an alternative to asking you questions if the pupils can gain the answer from a display; or to explore alternatives to hands up when you ask questions. Displays should therefore always link to pupils' learning. For example, there could be an image of a tree as a display and at the end of each day pupils could write what they have learnt on a green leaf and put it on the tree, and what they struggled with on a red or brown leaf, placing it at the bottom of the tree as if it had shed those leaves. You can then see instantly what needs to be revisited with some or all of the class and which pupils can move on in their learning. There are many different alternatives to this such as happy and sad faces, a flower or clouds, or different coloured boxes in which pupils can place their work.

In order to use display as an assessment tool, it must be interactive and offer different options. Ideally, you would plan for different individuals or groups to work with the display and observe their actions and learning, taking note of these. The success of pupils' learning rests purely on the effectiveness of the display. There is an alternative way in which display can be used as an assessment strategy for any curriculum subject – although very effective, this requires you to surrender the display to the pupils. You will prepare the background, borders and colours to be used, and pupils can then carefully plan their display to highlight their learning, be that pictorially, written or using photographs, artefacts or whatever they wish. As they will work in pairs or small groups, it supports the learning of all pupils. When the display is completed, you will be able to assess their understanding or knowledge by what they have done. Allowing pupils to display their learning provides them with ownership of their learning and offers you an opportunity to assess their learning, challenge their misunderstandings and correct their misconceptions.

Portfolios

Portfolios have been in education for many years as memory boxes and records of achievement. They are a tool for the collection and reflection of samples of pupils' work. They can either be samples of work already assessed, leading to judgements against age-related expectations, or can be used as a repository for pupils' work, illustrating progression in learning in specific subjects or areas of the curriculum. They could be said to be based on the records of achievement developed in the 1970s and 1980s and on the National Record of Achievement in 1991 with its comprehensive records of a pupil's life in and out of school (Black, 1998). In addition to individual portfolios, there may also be class or key stage portfolios that are used for moderation purposes. In this way, portfolios may be used to support new members of staff in levelling pupils against National Curriculum criteria. They can also be useful in demonstrating the standard of individual, class or key stage work to parents, governors of the school and trainee or newly qualified teachers (Stefani, *et al.* 2007). Pupils may be fully instrumental in the construction of their own portfolio, choosing the content to illustrate their thought processes and achievements. Pupils can gather data to provide a learning journey which includes personal reflections evidencing the ability to critically reflect on their learning (Klenowski, 2002), and there is increasing evidence that even pupils in early years are able to use portfolios effectively to support their learning (Carr, 2004). In this way, they

Context Sheet	Pupil Evaluation
Date: Brief description of sample collected: Illustrative nature of the sample: Signed:	Date: What is your work about? How well do you think you did it? What would you do differently next time? Signed:

Figure 9.1 Examples of context sheets

provide a rich source of data to support discussions between you, parents and pupils. One of the main considerations though is the criteria for selecting work and information to include, which can be driven by you as teacher or the pupil.

The advantages of pupils using a portfolio are that they can easily access their own learning, they have ownership of it and it encourages them to think about and reflect on their learning. Portfolios respond to the individual needs of the pupil, are organic and contain a celebration of their work that can, at defined times during the day, week or year, be shared with you and their parents. Portfolios encourage pupils to engage in understanding themselves as learners and offer them control and independence.

It is useful if each piece of work in the portfolio has a context sheet to explain who has collected the sample, when, why and what it illustrates (Butt, 2010). Asking pupils to evaluate their own work and include this in the portfolio can also be beneficial. You will need to decide, with or without input from pupils, how they can provide an illustrative sample of work in their portfolio. An example of a context sheet, which can be adapted for different age ranges, and of a pupil evaluation sheet are given in Figure 9.1.

Moving away from paper-based recording systems, e-portfolios are increasingly used in primary and secondary education, the use and merits of which are discussed further in Chapter 10.

Learning journals

A learning journal is a repository for reflection on learning and is very similar to the portfolio described above or to the web log or blog discussed in Chapter 10. It is a collection of notes, observations, thoughts and other relevant materials built up over a period of time. It is also known as a diary, log or learning log but it contains only reflections and no data (Moon, 1999). A learning journal contains the development and learning of a pupil and is completed at various times in the pupil's education, possibly over many years. Often, the contents are personal but this may not always be the case as a journal may include a conversation or a reflection on a joint activity. Contents may not always be on paper but can be voice-recorded or electronic. A learning journal can be simple and record the highlights of the day with a supporting reflective account. Alternatively, it could have 19 sections, such as that proposed by Progoff (1975). If learning journals were to be adopted in your classroom, I am sure you would opt for the simpler version.

The purpose of a learning journal is to enhance learning through the process of thinking about learning experiences (Moon, 2006). A learning journal is personal to the pupil and reflects the experiences, success and learning that have occurred. It can be constructed in any shape or form, from an extensive seven-year primary school record or an annual, termly, weekly or daily class record to a personal jotting on a plain piece of paper. The form it takes may be governed by the age of pupil you teach. Practitioners in the early years are likely to operate differently to those working in the later years of primary school. For example, very young pupils may represent their feelings about their learning through pictures such as happy and sad faces.

It is advisable that you impress on pupils that their journal is primarily for them but that you will ask them to share it with you at certain times, which is where your assessment of their learning fits in. From this, you will likely gain information not only on the learning that has taken place but also on the way in which pupils learn and their ability to reflect and engage with higher-order metacognition. Additionally, as always with primary pupils, there must be a purpose for asking them to engage with learning journals; they must see some point in doing this. They also need time apportioned for the learning journals to be completed. One suggestion might be that they could be used at the end of each day in a quiet reflective time before going home, similar to the leaves on a tree explained earlier in this chapter.

The advantages of learning journals are that they require reflective thinking and increased metacognition which are associated with deeper learning and increased outcomes for the pupil across the curriculum. They also offer opportunities for the pupil to revise what has been learnt, to ponder on any points of misunderstanding and to celebrate the successes of the day. They give you a tool to record pupils' experiences, develop their critical thinking and increase their active involvement, self-empowerment and ownership of their learning.

Reports

The aim of a report is to relay information or recount a set of events to a particular audience that can be public, private or individual. They can be used for different purposes such as to inform, describe, evaluate or explain something or to instruct, provoke or persuade (Bowden, 2008). They can use graphics, pictures, voice or specialised vocabulary, charts, tables, figures and hyperlinks, all of which pupils need to understand.

Report writing involves preparing a report so that you can assess whether pupils understand the language and format of reports compared with other genres of writing. In that way, reports may be represented as drama, role play or as a voice or video recording using a podcast or screencast, which are discussed further in Chapter 10. Reporting may be introduced by watching and listening to reports on television, with pupils noting the key words used. Similarly, this may be set as a homework task, presenting the findings on a mind or concept map. A good way for pupils to learn how to prepare a report is to listen to different types and understand that prior to these being broadcast there has been much planning and preparation. Reports are found in many different guises such as traffic reports, scientific reports, football match reports, inspection reports and pupils' annual reports. All use different language because they are aimed at different audiences and have different purposes. For example, you could not use the language of a traffic report for the annual report on a pupil's progress for parents any more than you could use a scientific report format for a traffic report. Therefore, when asking pupils to report, it is important to clarify the style of report, its purpose and the intended audience.

Finally, if the aim of the lesson is to assess whether pupils understand the language of reports, there should be no requirement for them to write this down. In fact, allowing pupils to work in small groups to decide on the type of report and then deliver this orally with support from visual display, computer graphics or resources of their choice could provide a stimulating activity from which you can assess whether they understand the nature of a report, the specialised language used, the tone and body language used and the ability to deliver to an audience. If you require them to write a report at a later date, pupils will have experience to draw on as they have first used drama to visualise the situation and it will therefore prove to be an easier task for them.

Points for Reflection

- Pupils think about learning in different ways to you or their parents.
- Pupils are learning all the time.
- Role play offers a safe place from which difficult concepts can be explored.
- There are different ways in which you can use posters and displays to assess pupils.
- Ownership and purpose are the key issues when developing portfolios.
- Portfolios develop pupils' strategies for thinking about their work.

Further Reading

Aldridge, M. (2003) *Meeting the Early Learning Goals through Role Play*. London: David Fulton.

Bowden, J. (1996) *How to Write a Report: A Step by Step Guide to Effective Report Writing*. Plymouth: How To Books.

Brice, T. (2010) *Learning through Play: Babies, Toddlers and the Foundation Years*. Dubai: Hodder Education.

Carr, M. (2001) *Assessment in Early Childhood Settings: Learning Stories*. London: SAGE.

CHAPTER 10

THE USE OF ICT IN ASSESSMENT

Chapter Objectives

1 To consider wider use of ICT in the classroom
2 To understand how ICT can be assessed through a variety of subjects and activities
3 To understand how other subjects can be assessed through ICT
4 To be able to engage with some of the suggestions in this chapter regarding the different possible uses for ICT in the classroom

Technology to enhance assessment

The use of technology both inside and outside the classroom has developed rapidly since the introduction of the interactive whiteboard into classrooms at the turn of the twenty-first century. The development of a range of mobile devices which are smaller but have more power and the emergence of digital technologies have offered the possibility of extending classroom e-learning. Speed, automation, capacity and range have improved and developed so that e-learning assessment is now considered one of the most important ways in which to raise attainment (Beauchamp, 2012). It is likely that pupils will enter school with experience of a number of technological devices that as a young child you possibly did not. Few people, though, would disagree that ICT is an important skill in preparing pupils for modern life. It is used in schools by teachers to enhance teaching and learning and assessment, and by secretarial staff who embrace it to improve the organisation and efficient working of schools. Of course, integrating information and communication technology (ICT) into the primary curriculum depends totally on the resources available in your school and the expertise of the staff in using it. Similarly, pupils will have differing capabilities as not every household has a computer or access to the internet. Successful integration of ICT across the curriculum takes both planning and preparation but offers an opportunity for assessing subject knowledge and understanding of all National Curriculum subjects including ICT as a discrete skill.

E-assessment

The word e-portfolio seems to have grown out of three different assessment activities that can be captured by e-portfolios: Computer Based Assessment (CBA), Computer Assisted Assessment (CAA) and Computer Moderated Assessment (CMA) (Butt, 2010). In the present climate of considerable technological change, it seems as though most assessments and records of pupils could increasingly move towards e-assessment such as the e-portfolio, where all documents are stored electronically.

ICT is already in use within primary schools for a range of reasons such as Assessing Pupil Progress (APP) and it is important that you are critically aware of the strengths and limitations of the different types of e-assessment, which need to be more efficient, more flexible and at least as robust and valid as paper assessment methods. In essence, e-assessment needs to do what paper assessment cannot do, in particular storing large amounts of data. E-assessment can be used for a range of activities such as asking questions and setting tasks, sorting, storing and distributing students' work. One of the advantages of this is that it is 'motivational and engaging' (Butt, 2010: 111). He suggests that e-assessment can provide hints, prompts and alternative ways in which to solve problems, although arguably being able to use this efficiently requires a very good knowledge of ICT. E-assessment offers the opportunity for diagnosis through an examination of the problem-solving processes used by the pupil and is therefore assessing the process of learning as well as the outcome.

It is likely that most schools now operate a virtual learning environment (VLE) which stores much information including contacts, events, assessment or attendance information. However, it relies on pupils having access to computers at home and having the same operating system as the school. Many software packages for VLEs offer a range of assessment practices such as multiple choice and 'drag and drop' which can offer instant feedback to the pupil (Rynne, 2009). Similarly, handheld devices can be used to register pupils' responses to questions or problems. With the response analysis being displayed on a computer screen, it is simple for you to assess the understanding and knowledge of pupils in the particular topic you are teaching. Similarly, digital capture pens, personal desktop assistants (PDAs), smartphones, tablets and iPads can be used not only to complete set tasks but also to gather photographic, sound, video and artistic information or evidence of pupils' learning.

E-portfolios can be a combination of any of the above e-assessment processes but are used particularly to integrate both learning and assessment, allowing the pupil to become more autonomous in the recording and monitoring process. They support both personal development and reflective learning. An advantage is that the e-portfolio can be accessed by pupils, parents and you as the teacher. It allows the pupil to learn 'how, where and when they wish' (Butt, 2010). E-portfolios work in the same way as paper-based portfolios (discussed in Chapter 7), being depositories for records of learning, exemplar work and any other records of achievement within and outside the National Curriculum. E-portfolios also have the advantage that they are easily transferable should the pupil move schools or transfer to secondary education.

An e-portfolio can be used as a tool for learning that can evidence learning in knowledge, skills, understanding and professional skills but also indicate reflection on that learning. If learning is to take place, then it is important that pupils can easily access the technology used as the repository for the e-portfolio. Similarly, pupil motivation for its use will depend on their understanding of its purpose which should be clearly explained to them. Is it an official record of their work or an optional activity? Who owns it and who has access to it? If used well, e-portfolios encourage self-reflection, can cater for a wide range of learning styles and offer an opportunity for starting the journey to lifelong learning.

As well as being used as a learning tool, e-portfolios can assess progress. It may be that the e-portfolio has several parts such as evidencing the learning, the reflections and the assessments. Alternatively, as long as you have access to the e-portfolios, then you can monitor progress and formerly assess the learning evidenced in the e-portfolio at certain times during the week or unit of work. Wherever there is a learning opportunity, there is also an assessment opportunity which should be seized by you as the teacher. In addition to e-portfolios, there are a range of different technologies that can now be used as assessment tools. These include: digital cameras, Flickr, wikis, blogs, podcasting and screencasting, which are all briefly described below.

With any technology, it is important to ensure that pupils are safe from online exploitation. Whereas school computers are required by the Child Internet Protection Act to filter content, if pupils are expected to continue, for example, the wiki or blog at home, there may be no such protection on their home computers. Therefore, it may be a good idea to ensure pupils and parents are Child Exploitation and On-Line Protection (CEOP) trained and fully aware of the dangers before using online technologies.

The next sections of this chapter look at different software tools that are available for use in primary schools. These are, in general, communication or collaboration devices that offer opportunities to link in with a wide base of knowledge and assess pupils' learning.

Blogs

Originally, blogs were lists of internet sites a person had visited on a particular day but today they comprise conversations, thoughts and reflections and can be updated whenever the user wishes (Dyrud et al., 2005). Modern blogs require interaction and they engage readers with ideas or questions that require a response. They are very much like a diary in that they are chronologically ordered and can be enhanced with images, text, video, audio and even games. After social networking, blogging is the most frequently used digital source (Barber and Cooper, 2012). Blog entries are normally within the same field of expertise or interest but a blog is not necessarily a personal account. Many blogs have a large audience of professional or personal contacts. A blog entry is instantly published and can be used with any age group in primary school.

Within the school environment, there is evidence that blogs can deepen learning (Richardson, 2009). They can be used as a class portal, an online filing cabinet or a collaborative space. As a class portal, they can be used to communicate information about the class, the lesson or homework and to archive resources and presentations used in lessons. Blogs can motivate learners and encourage reluctant readers (Hufflaker, 2004). They are a forum for interaction and can be an extension of the classroom learning environment. If parents also have access to the blog, they can easily check on the content of lessons and see if their child has any homework! Using a blog as an online filing cabinet can help work towards the classroom becoming a paperless zone. Pupils post their work online for you to respond to. It ensures that they do not lose their work, it saves their work into one place and it can be shared with others in collaborative learning. It is this collaborative space that is the real advantage of blogs. Pupils can learn from each other, from scientists, researchers or other professionals and it is the potential audience that makes blogs an effective constructivist learning strategy. This idea may require a different way of thinking about how the primary classroom is organised, with the ability to collaborate with other classrooms that can share information through text, picture, sound or film. Blogs can be used to archive the teaching and learning within the classroom, enabling much more reflection and metacognitive examination than was previously viable. Additionally, because blogs can accommodate a range of learning styles, they can reach pupils who are reluctant learners or who have writing difficulties. Depending on how you, as the teacher, integrate the blog, pupils can take ownership of their space, which encourages them to become increasingly independent learners. As a teacher, you can also use a blog to collaborate with subject specialists to support your own professional development by evaluating the information for validity.

As with everything in teaching, it is important that you plan carefully – in this case, you need to plan how you and your pupils are going to engage with blogs. It may be that to begin with you just post homework tasks on the blog and respond to this when completed by the pupil, teaching pupils and their parents how to access this at home. Next, you may choose certain weblogs with suitable content for the age of pupil you are teaching and provide a model they can follow until they are confident enough to respond to the posts themselves.

Having the information on the blog makes assessment different than on paper but, with experience, blogging may become an easier option as it will save you carrying many books home for marking as you can tap into pupils' blogs wherever you are. When you assess pupils' work, you will also be able to access the internet to offer support and examples of how they can improve. This will save you time as it saves reinventing the wheel when information is already in cyberspace. Offering ways for pupils to improve is the best way to further their learning.

Wikis

A wiki is an expandable collection of web pages with a hypertext system for modifying the data and where content can be directly linked to other information online (Augar et al., 2004). Wikis are fully editable websites and anyone can read, reorganise or update the wiki as they wish. No special software is needed and content is uploaded immediately. In effect, they are communities of practice that share common interests and knowledge through a constructivist learning environment. The founder of Wikipedia, Jimmy Wales, stated his reason for developing it was the idea that every person in the world should have free access to the sum of all human knowledge (Wales, 2004). Wikipedia is an encyclopaedia of information to which new information is added daily. However, one drawback is that there is no check that the information posted is accurate and authors are anonymous, so wikis must be used with caution. However, a wiki is slightly different to Wikipedia. The word originates from Hawaii where the word *wiki wiki* means 'quick' (Richardson, 2009). Wikis are, therefore, a place where anonymous people get together to create knowledge. Wikis can be in 'read' or 'edit' mode but are left in read mode as default.

Within the classroom, wikis can encourage collaborative learning such as a group of pupils building a factfile of information on the effect of greenhouse gases; mummification; life in the Second World War; or any number of topics, and printing this out to become part of the learning journal (Axel and Humphreys, 2005). For example, different groups may investigate and create their wiki on aspects of life in the Victorian era such as dress, food, housing and childhood. This would provide a useful resource for a topic on the Victorians and you would be able to assess pupils' knowledge and understanding of life in Victorian times by what was included in the wiki and how they disseminated this to the rest of the class. There is also an opportunity to assess social skills through the use of wikis as pupils need to collaborate, negotiate and discuss the entries they make. The discussion board of a wiki is a teaching and learning tool in that there is an immediate audience who can extend the resources, comment on the content and discuss issues, all of which enhance learning (Leuf and Cunningham, 2001). Learning and assessment in the wiki world is collaborative and entails communicating ideas and knowledge through a digital environment, and collaboration or constructivism is the most effective way of deep learning (Palloff and Pratt, 1999).

To start using a wiki, you will need to access a site such as Wikispaces (www.wikispaces.com) which is the most popular site for classroom teachers. From here you can create an account, choosing a 'protected' wiki. You can add audio or video to your page, upload pictures or files and add subpages. Wikispaces also has the capability for pupils to add reflections on their work or to add to, or negotiate to remove, the content of the page. Each pupil may also have their own wiki page which you can monitor, and use for adding teaching resources and for assessing content and reflections on learning.

Flickr

Flickr (www.flickr.com) is an image-hosting website that gives you the option to create and publish content other than text with digital cameras. At its simplest, a digital camera can be used by the teacher as a teaching tool. Images taken of the work pupils produce or of the way in which pupils are collaborating can easily be uploaded onto the classroom computer and used as a future teaching tool or as part of the plenary to revise and assess pupils' work. An advantage of Flickr is that it offers an opportunity for you to add notes to part of a photograph so that you can use this as a teaching tool. Similarly, you could be the catalyst for discussion about a digital photograph and assess pupils' reactions to and reflections on this, all of which can be held in private with access given only to you and your class. This is another technology that can be used safely and has the potential to motivate students as it is a different learning strategy. As an assessment strategy, there is the ability to access pupils' work from wherever you are and to leave formative comments.

Podcasting and screencasting

A podcast is an audio recording that can be distributed via the World Wide Web and enable learning at any time. The word 'pod' originates from the acronym POD which means 'playable on demand' (Hammersley, 2004). The suffix 'cast', as in broadcast, relates to the transmission of media content. As with on-demand television, a podcast can be stored and listened to whenever it is convenient. Most podcasts are short in length and may be homemade or relate to a television or radio programme. They cannot link to other podcasts and in this way they differ from wikis and blogs, although you can upload a podcast, wiki or blog. Podcasting is therefore a less social activity unless you require pupils to create podcasts in collaboration. Podcasts are a powerful way in which to convey attitudes, feelings and viewpoints (Ormond, 2008). They are less useful for transmitting facts and details. A podcast cannot replace you or your classroom teaching, learning and assessment but can provide a further opportunity to tap into different styles of pupils' learning, as they spend much of their time outside school using technology. Podcasts can be used as additional support for pupils or can be a repository where you access and assess learning. Podcasts are especially helpful in that pupils can easily pause and replay content they may not fully understand on first hearing. They are also useful for supporting different learning styles, pupils with English as an additional language and pupils with SEN. From an assessment point of view, you can evaluate what pupils produce following your podcast. You may set them the task of creating a podcast in response to your podcast. You can listen to and assess their answers, their thought processes and their ICT skills through their responses to your podcasts and the creation of their own.

In order to create a podcast, you will need the means to digitally record audio and convert it to an MP3 file format; you will also need something to say. If pupils have their own or a school-owned iPad, they too can access learning via podcasts, easily creating podcasts themselves, recounting their learning, their research or their reflections. You can then access the podcast to assess pupils' work. This is another inclusive practice as there is no requirement to write and it can be used across all curriculum subjects. If you create a podcast, pupils could then follow up their learning by writing responses to your podcast, which would allow you to assess both their listening and writing levels and their use of ICT.

A further development of podcasting is screencasting, which captures what you and your pupils do on a computer screen adding a narration. You could create screencasts as support for pupils when teaching complex ICT skills or possibly gymnastics or dance movements so that a narrative can be added that either describes the movement or perhaps critically appraises it. Through this medium, pupils can annotate their work in voice, create a visual accompaniment for a piece of poetry or offer their feelings on a story they have read or listened to. Because in screencasting you are combining visual and audio files, it is slightly more complicated than podcasting. However, the potential is much greater as it can assess and provide feedback on the progress of pupils in subjects across the National Curriculum, whereby action and narration are used in conjunction.

To conclude, the advancement of technology in the twenty-first century is rapid and part of your role as a teacher is to explore and use an increasing variety of technological features to assess pupils. In addition to being able to assess any part of the curriculum, you can constantly evaluate pupils' ICT skills, knowledge and understanding as they successfully interact with an increasing number of modern technologies safely available for primary-aged pupils. At present, there is a World Wide Web that will inevitably grow and be increasingly used by teachers who realise its potential to enhance the learning, teaching and assessment of all pupils.

Points for Reflection

- The potential for e-assessment is high with vast benefits for pupils, parents, governors and you as the teacher.
- E-assessment can encourage pupils to become more autonomous and personalised in their learning.
- E-assessment has the capacity to store large amounts of data that can be filtered in order to ease access to specific information.
- The success of e-assessment depends on the availability of training and resources and a commitment from the whole-school community.
- E-assessment is only the preferred method if its benefits outweigh those of the paper version.

Further Reading

Aldrich, D., Bell, B. and Batzel, T. (2006) *Automated Podcasting Solution Expands the Boundaries of the Classroom*. Edmonton, CA: SIGUCCCS.

Copley, J. (2007) 'Audio and Video Podcasts of Lectures for Campus-Based Students: Production and Evaluation of Student Use', *Innovations in Education and Teaching International*, 44(4): 387–99.

Cress, U. and Kimmerle, J. (2008) 'A Systematic and Cognitive View on Collaborative Knowledge Building with Wikis', *Computer-Supported Collaborative Learning*, 3: 105–22.

De-Cicco, E., Farmer, M. and Hargrave, C. (1999) *Activities for Using the Internet in Primary Schools*. London: Kogan Page.

Duffty, J. (2006) *Extending Knowledge in Practice: Primary ICT*. Exeter: Learning Matters.

Lamb, B. (2004) 'Wide Open Spaces: Wikis, Ready or Not', *EDUCAUSE Review*, 39(5): 36–48.

Poore, M. (2012) *Using Social Media in the Classroom*. London: SAGE.

Raitman, R., Augar, N. and Zhou, W. (2005) 'Employing Wikis for Online Collaboration in the E-Learning Environment: Case Study'. Proceedings of the Third International Conference on Information Technology and Applications, Sydney, NSW, July.

Selwyn, N., Potter, J. and Cranmer, S. (2010) *Primary Schools and ICT: Learning from Pupil Perspectives*. London: Continuum.

Weiler, G. (2003) 'Using Weblogs in the Classroom', *The English Journal*, 92(5): 73–5.

CHAPTER 11

FEEDBACK, RECORDING AND REPORTING

Chapter Objectives

1 To understand the importance of oral and written feedback as assessment strategies to promote learning
2 To understand how target setting is linked to feedback and forms part of the teaching, learning and assessment cyclical process
3 To consider a range of ways in which to store pupil records
4 To understand the statutory duties of teachers relating to assessment, recording and reporting

The final chapter of the book explores how feedback and target setting as assessment strategies promote learning. It offers different ways in which you can record assessments and details the statutory duties relating to assessment, recording and reporting to which you must adhere, including the annual report on the progress of pupils to their parents.

Marking

The need to make decisions is perhaps one of the most important characteristics of a teacher's role and you will make numerous decisions in the classroom throughout each day, often on the spur of the moment, based on what you see, hear or observe. These informal decisions are assessments that you make and far outnumber the more formal assessments that you may plan, possibly because they occur without prior planning. However, if you want specific information then formal assessment must be planned, although this can take place how, when and where you choose. Perhaps the most well-known assessment strategy is marking.

The word *marking* derives from an old German word, *marcon*, which had the meaning of setting out a boundary to delineate one person's land from another. Although the word marking now has a much wider meaning, summative tests that are graded still have boundaries or grading levels (Wragg, 2001). If the word marking is taken in its wider sense, it relates to feeding back to pupils the successes of their work. If pupils are to learn from their work, then it is essential to report on their work positively. Marking is a complex process concerned with communication between you and the pupil or between one pupil and another. Pupils should be able to understand what you or their peers mean by the comments made. You are able to decide the purpose of your marking, for example whether pupils have completed the task or acted on the advice you offered after the last session, or whether the specific learning objectives have been achieved. It is difficult to divorce yourself from marking for accountability to parents, the head teacher or Ofsted; nevertheless it is important to remember that your first accountability is to each pupil in your class and if you keep this as a focus then you should succeed in ensuring the feedback you provide supports pupils' learning. Therefore, it is useful to think about which errors to correct, what type of comments to write, where these should be written and how to follow up in ensuring that pupils have learnt from their errors. If marking relates specifically to a set of pre-determined learning objectives, then it should be positive, precise and specific.

Ideally, marking involves feedback to the pupil that offers an assessment of the current situation and ways to improve. Marking can have different purposes such as communication, recognition of work completed, monitoring understanding or knowledge or motivation and target setting. For example, you may just want to acknowledge that a specific item has been addressed with a tick or simple comment. This is the least refined type of feedback, offering little information to the pupil. On the other hand, marking can be useful and informative for the pupil by offering a clear indication of what has been achieved and what the pupil should do next in order to improve. This type of marking is motivational and is based on constructive criticism that directly relates the pupil's work to the learning outcomes. Often, this can be achieved by using the 3:1 principle which requires three positive comments and one target for improvement. It is often called *three stars and a wish* or something similar. You can record assessment by a variety of means such as ticks, crosses, smiley faces, grades or written comments. These are diverse rationales but as you will spend much time marking, it is essential that you avoid focusing your time on marking that has little value and are confident that the time spent has been informative to both you and the pupil. It is not essential to provide a written comment on everything pupils do as this would be time-consuming and would possibly result in ineffective marking. Identify clearly what you want to assess from the learning outcomes and comment only on that. For example, if you want to assess pupils' understanding of a historical timeline, there should be no need to correct spellings or sentence construction, although this is perhaps easier said than done. Similarly, in writing, if your focus from the learning objectives is the use of a range of adjectives to describe a giant, then it is not important if the pupil misses a full stop or capital letter here or there. A key factor in marking is that it should be integral to the lesson rather than an afterthought bolted on at the end of the lesson.

Unfortunately, research indicates that marking is often directly responsible for the regression of pupils, is demoralising and is unintelligible to pupils (Clarke, 2001). To be effective, marking in whatever form it takes should be planned, linked to the learning objectives, help pupils identify and address their misconceptions, provide ways in which pupils can improve, be fit for purpose and useful, and happen soon after the work has been completed in order that pupils remember the focus of the teaching and their task related to this. Focused marking can result in increased self-esteem and self-efficacy, increased motivation and pupils becoming more independent in knowing how to close the gap and work towards their targets. It can also benefit you, as your marking clearly evidences improvement in pupils' learning, there is a purpose to your marking and it should focus you on the learning objectives rather than on secretarial issues such as punctuation and spelling. Feedback on pupils' work has the power to support and improve pupils' attainment and it is therefore important that it is executed effectively. A key issue relating to any form of feedback is how pupils react to it and the subsequent impact on their motivation for future learning. To minimise negative reactions, pupils need to be provided with information on what they did well and what they can do to improve. Marking and feedback will take up a considerable amount of your time and therefore you should aim to be as effective as possible by considering why, what and how you are marking, through prioritisation and by adopting a range of alternative assessment techniques, such as those that have been discussed in this book. Effective feedback will create deeper thinking, increase reflection and provide a way forward for the pupil but it has to be manageable for you. Ideally, you need to aim for marking less, but marking more effectively.

Feedback

Effective feedback depends solely on your precise and accurate assessment of a pupil's learning so that you and the pupil have a clear understanding of the successes and areas for development, and so that you understand their preferences as a learner and can set future targets for their learning. It is a necessary part of the marking process in that without some form of feedback pupils will not know how well they have done nor how they may improve for the future. Gradually, a pupil can become more empowered and self-directed in setting their own targets and in supporting their own learning. Pupils also need feedback that is positive and encouraging so that it has an emotional and academic impact. The important point about any feedback is that it needs to be clear to the pupil what they need to do in order to improve and reach their targets. Pupils will often need support in closing the gap between what they have achieved and their target. This may take the form of modelling, questioning, instructing or collaboration between pupils.

Feedback is personal and pupils can react and respond to it in different ways; it is your responsibility to ensure that pupils' reactions are positive and motivational as you know their personalities. It is the knowledge you have of pupils' emotional readiness for learning, your sensitivity to their needs and your timing of the feedback that can be key to pupils viewing critical feedback as ways to improve, rather than it being seen as something negative, and ensuring that they focus on what they can do rather than on what they cannot. Effective feedback is the most powerful form of raising attainment (Clarke, 2001) if it encourages intrinsic motivation and confidence and offers the pupil ownership and control of their learning (Broadfoot, 2007). The greatest motivation for a pupil derives from feedback that concentrates on their work rather than on a comparison of their work with that of other pupils in the class (Crooks, 2001). Successful feedback will increase self-esteem, create improved performance and be a positive learning experience.

Oral feedback

Oral feedback is the most powerful force for moving pupils on in their learning (Clarke, 2001) because it allows pupils to clarify misconceptions immediately. Of course, the ability to provide manageable and effective oral feedback relies on the classroom organisation and your ability to focus on individuals or small groups of pupils rather than the whole class.

Oral feedback can be direct or indirect and ideally should be implicit in all lessons. It takes time to develop, needs to be planned and requires fostering in a supportive environment. It can be between teacher and pupil; pupil and pupil; or pupil and teacher. The advantages of oral feedback are that it is immediate, adaptable, ongoing, episodic, stimulating, personalised, versatile and motivating. Sometimes, though, instant responses may not be well considered, pupils may not take oral feedback seriously, pupils may feel exposed or they may not have the time to reflect on what has been said because time is limited. With lower-ability pupils, it is important that oral feedback does not provide answers but challenges them to find the solutions themselves through you signposting the way.

As with any feedback, it is important that your comments are specific, measurable, relevant and achievable. For example, the following remarks do not provide any indication of what can be improved nor how to improve it:

- You are not making the most of working in a group (Why not? How do I make the most of it?).
- I do not think you have got the foreground right (Why not? I do not know how to do this).
- Well done, a constructive answer (In what way? Was it the right answer or just a constructive one?).
- You need to ensure you use the same volume of liquid (Why? How do I do this?).
- An interesting story, but you could develop it further (If I knew how maybe I could, but I do not know how).

As you can see, these teacher responses are not clear. If they were, then pupils would not still have questions to ask; rather, pupils should be taken on to the next steps in their learning. Alternative comments might be:

- If you listen to what the other people in your group are saying, you could join in with your ideas.
- If you look at this picture you can see that the foreground is larger than buildings further away so you could try to make the houses in the foreground larger than those further away.
- Your answer was constructive in that it made Sam feel good about his suggestion and he now knows how to continue to construct his boat so that it floats.
- In a fair test you must keep one thing stable at all times which will provide you with more consistent results. What is the constant in your experiment?
- Your story is interesting but if you had developed the characters more it would have been more exciting. Try to do this next time.

Therefore, plan oral feedback which is positive and specific, reinforce the value and importance of pupils' contribution, focus feedback on the learning objectives and success criteria, give pupils time to reflect and respond, encourage pupils to ask questions to clarify understanding, identify and agree next steps, revising pupil targets if necessary, agree longer-term actions, clarify when these will be reviewed, by whom and what evidence will be needed. It is also important to use 'no blame' language such as in the following examples:

> What do we need to remember here?
> I know you can…
> Which part did I not explain well enough?
> Lots of people get muddled on this bit.
> OK, no worries, you haven't quite mastered it yet.
> Up to now this has been a little tricky.
> You will remember when…
> You choose…

Oral feedback can be used for different purposes. Look at Figure 11.1 and note down which of the examples you use or have observed in other classrooms and how well these strategies worked.

Purpose	Example of feedback
Correcting an error	Good try but let's look at it again
Providing information	Yes, the word you are looking for is …
Appraising and praising	Good thinking, that is a good idea
Challenging	Try again but this time …
Seeking clarification	What did you mean by this bit?
Encouraging exploration, elaboration or development	Which would be the best way to …? How might you develop that idea?
Redirecting learning	That is a detailed illustration. Now move on to …
Focusing learning	All this is important but your work would be better if …
Confirming and moving learning forward	Yes that is right, now can you …
Agreeing next steps	So think now about two changes you might make to improve …
Distilling and summarising learning	Let's revise what we have learnt so far …
Encouraging reflection	Let's think about what we have discussed; what else might we need to do?
Focusing on learning strategies	Excellent, how did you manage to improve …?

Figure 11.1 Types of oral feedback

Types of oral feedback

Of course, these are only a few examples and in your professional experience you will encounter a large range of purposes for offering oral feedback.

Written feedback

This is perhaps the most frequent form of feedback offered to pupils in primary school but, according to Ofsted reports (2008a, 2010), written feedback is variable in its quality and impact on pupils' learning. The Ofsted reports indicate that the quality of teachers' marking varies too much. At its best, marking provides a personal response to pupils' work which helps to increase their confidence and clearly identifies areas for improvement; at its worst, it is time-consuming, unfocused and of little use to the teacher or pupil. The reports suggest that in many lessons that were observed, marking typically focused on presentation, quantity of work, effort involved or surface features such as spelling, grammar and punctuation. The conclusions were that most teachers now share the lesson's learning objectives with pupils but that feedback relates to effort or quality of work produced rather than to the learning objectives themselves. This is not to say that effort, quality or presentation should not be rewarded in another way but they should not specifically interfere with assessment of the learning objectives unless they form part of them.

Although written feedback can range from a tick or grade to extensive written comments, research (Black et al., 2003) suggests that if there is a grade and written comments, pupils focus on the grade alone and fail to read the comments. Black et al. (2003) continue to suggest that grades provide short-term rewards and little information on how to improve, particularly if the extrinsic reward is seen as a sort of bribe and leads to pupils failing to choose activities that do not have such extrinsic rewards (Lepper and Hodell, 1989). Short-term extrinsic rewards foster pupils striving for the reward not the achievement, and encourage competition not cooperation. Pupils of average ability get the fewest rewards and such rewards only offer pupils short-term motivational gains. Therefore, it is better for you to write comments only and allow time for pupils to read and act on the advice you have offered.

One disadvantage of making written comments on pupils' work is the workload it may generate, which is perhaps why the Ofsted reports above suggest that comments on pupils' work are often generic in nature and provide no real information to the pupil on achievements gained or ways to improve. Try to think of other ways to assess pupils, such as those that have been discussed earlier in this book, that do not require either the pupils or you to write significant amounts. You may, for example, choose to increase the amount of oral feedback you give, noting down only the most significant advances or improvements.

However, sometimes marking, as oral feedback above, fails to tell pupils how they can improve and tends towards indiscriminate praise. It is often plagued with arbitrary comments or comments that are not fully expounded. Consider the following and judge their effectiveness:

- Develop these ideas further – which and how?
- More detail needed – on what?
- You must try harder – why? I tried as hard as I could.

- Ask... – what about?
- A lovely story – but was it good?
- Good work – what was good?
- Spellings – what about them?
- Use paragraphs – I would if I knew how.
- A good attempt – so, what did I do well and what did I not do well?

As you have probably noticed, all the above phrases are vague in that pupils do not know what or how they can improve.

In order for feedback to be positive and useful, it needs to ensure that the learning objectives and success criteria are specific. Comments should relate to the learning objectives, be specific, offer ways in which the pupil can improve and ensure the balance of comments is positive by applying the *three stars and a wish* principle, allowing the pupil time to read and act on the feedback you have provided (Dix, 2010). Effective feedback will focus on the learning objectives and success criteria, as explained earlier in this book, will confirm pupils are on the right track, stimulate the correction of errors or improvement, scaffold pupils' next steps, provide opportunities for pupils to extend thinking, comment on progress made, avoid comparisons with other pupils and provide pupils with the opportunity to respond. In order to close the gap between what pupils know now and what you want them to know in the future, you need to provide comments so that they understand their mistakes and offer strategies for them to improve. There are three sorts of prompts that can be used in feedback to promote further learning:

- *Reminder prompts* draw the pupil back to the learning objectives and success criteria of the lesson.
- *Scaffold prompts* ask questions that will specifically encourage the pupil to meet the learning objectives and will either begin a sentence for a pupil to finish, write a cloze sentence for the pupil to finish or bullet point the necessary additions.
- *Example prompts* provide a couple of example sentences for the pupil to choose from or write their own based on your example.

For example, if the context of the lesson was to write a story about a naughty dog and the learning objective was to express a character's feelings, a reminder prompt may ask: how do you think the dog felt at this point in the story? A scaffold prompt may ask the pupil to describe the expression on the dog's face by offering part sentences: He was so ... he ...; he barked _____ly running round feeling very _____. An example prompt may offer the pupil a choice of two sentences or to write their own sentence like the ones provided: He ran around in circles looking for the rabbit, feeling very confused; He was very sad because…

You can check the effectiveness of your feedback by considering whether: your comments relate to the learning objectives and success criteria; they will promote the pupil's self-esteem; the selected piece of assessment represents a milestone in the pupil's learning; the next steps for improvement are identified and new challenges are set; and you have provided a closing the gap prompt to support the future learning of the pupil. Future learning goals can also be referred to as targets.

Target setting

A target is defined as a goal, an aim or an aspiration which suggests that it is something yet to be achieved. Targets use sources of information to focus plans on raising attainment to ensure pupils' prior achievements are built on. A target should identify and focus on teaching and areas of underperformance, be information gathering, identify achievements and next steps with specific actions and usually be part of a school's annual improvement plan. Targets can be numerical or expressed in words and can be set by the government, by the local authorities, by senior managers in your school or by you as the teacher.

Statutory target setting was introduced in England and Wales in 1988 with the introduction of the first modern National Curriculum (DfES, 1988). Data on pupils' achievements based on their targets must be submitted annually and is analysed by various organisations, such as the DfE, Ofsted and the Fischer Family Trust, and provided to the school during the autumn term each year. As these results can hold teachers and governors to account, it is important that the targets set are challenging but realistic and achievable within a set time frame. You will also find that there is a target focus on underachieving pupils, pupils with English as an additional language and pupils with SEN.

There are three parts to target setting for pupils: quantitative tracking, individual pupil qualitative targets and targets that are not recorded. Quantitative targets are those often recorded electronically. It is a number-crunching exercise that allows the tracking of pupil progress against National Curriculum targets which are gathered from SATs or the optional tests available throughout the school and will identify whether or not pupils are on track to achieve age-related expectations. Target setting should include not only test scores but also the wealth of information you have as the teacher about each pupil's achievements. Qualitative targets are opinions on the achievement of pupil progress that can be measured against National Curriculum programmes of study, against the other pupils in the class or against the pupil's own previous performances. Setting targets based on pupils' previous achievements also increases motivation and self-esteem (Clarke, 2001). Non-recorded targets are those often set by the pupils themselves during self-evaluation sessions. Additionally, focused marking can result in pupils setting their own targets that are based on their performance in lessons.

Targets must be based on pupils' prior attainment, focus on improvement and provide ways in which the pupil will achieve through a commitment by both the pupil and yourself. Setting targets is a well-known strategy for raising the attainment of a school. Typically, there will be a top-down focus on target setting. This means that the government sets targets which are passed down to local authorities, then on to schools, key stages, classes and pupils. Ideally, target setting should be bottom-up, starting with the needs of each pupil. There is also the issue of who sets, monitors and assesses the success of achieving the target. If target setting is to be effective, then it needs to have a purpose and direction that the pupil can follow. Otherwise, the targets drive the teaching rather than the learning, which then takes little account of the needs of each pupil. Initially, target setting will be largely initiated by you, although as pupils become more aware of the process of target setting the responsibility should shift towards the pupil also setting their own targets through self-assessment.

Targets can have different names such as challenges or missions (Dix, 2010) and be written in pupils' books, on laminated cards, on stickers, on desks, on the wall in the form of a display (see Chapter 9) or can take the form of a tree or flower that grows each time a target is achieved or the form of a children's heroic character such as Superman or Wonder Woman. If pupils are stimulated by the targets, in whichever form you choose to display them, this should encourage pupils to work towards them. All targets should be specific, measureable, achievable, relevant and time limited, providing the opportunity for pupils to reflect on and evaluate their successes and eventually work towards setting their own future targets.

Accurate target setting underpins all successful assessment. If pupils are clear about their targets and know what they need to do to achieve them, parents are fully aware of their child's targets and you are confident and have high expectations of each pupil, then assessments and future target setting should form a major part of the assessment cycle. Ideally, targets should directly feed into your teaching and pupils' learning.

Recording

Recording is a tool which aids you in remembering significant events, learning and interactions in your pupils' day. You may record what pupils learn, how they do it, their interactions with other pupils, their behaviour and their motivation for learning. As raw data, this serves no purpose; it is only when you analyse these situations that you can affect the future learning of the pupils in your class.

There are many assessments that take place in primary school every day and, working within school policy, it will be up to you to decide what, when and where this recording happens. It is important to understand which assessments should be kept, how the information will be used and where assessments will be stored. Much information relating to the assessment of pupils in your class will be carried around in your head. But at some point at least, some of this information needs recording more formally. If used effectively, recording a pupil's achievements will enhance their learning. Butt (2010) suggests that there are three purposes to recording pupil achievement: to record key milestones in pupil learning, to monitor progress and set future targets or to inform other people such as parents. You must decide what to record and ensure that this is manageable and informative. If too much time is spent on assessing pupils, then teaching receives less time. You need to think of the value of the assessments you record and whether they provide useful information on pupil performance. The recording you make for your information will be different to the feedback you provide for pupils as they have different purposes. Assessments can be recorded in different ways – as percentages, as levels, in prose or as an average, in mark or grade books or on the computer – however, you must consider whether these are informative. It may be better to include bigger boxes on the computer or in a mark book that provide succinct but valuable information on each pupil rather than a symbol or number. The key issue is to decide on the purpose of and audience for the records you make and whether they are an effective and efficient way of providing you with the rich information you need to ensure each pupil is challenged with appropriate targets. Your school will probably have an assessment policy; if so, it is essential that you read the policy and speak with the assessment coordinator to understand your responsibilities in assessing and recording the work of pupils in your class. The way you choose to record pupil progress should provide the basis for the conversations you have with pupils and for the reports you provide to parents, senior managers and the teacher due to take over your class at the start of the next academic year.

Reporting

Reporting is a significant part of the assessment process which deals with communicating the assessments you have made to a range of stakeholders. It can be formative, such as that you may provide for the pupil, for the teacher taking over your class at the start of the academic year or for parents who wish to support their child's learning at home. Alternatively, it may be summative, such as that required by local authorities and central government. At certain stages in primary school, you are required to provide National Curriculum levels or other data such as the results of pupils' EYFS Profiles or Reading by Six. However, pupils, parents and central government do not share the same understanding of the content nor the context within which the teaching and learning has taken place, nor necessarily understand the language or educational jargon used. Additionally, external moderators may visit the school to verify your assessments or to check on the security of national tests.

Reporting progress to pupils helps them to understand their successes and their next targets for improvement. Reporting to parents involves them in better understanding the teaching process and allows them to identify the progress made since the last report. Reporting to the next teacher ensures the continuity and progression of pupils' learning, and reporting to local authorities or central government allows them to compare pupil achievement in your school with similar schools and schools in the top-performance quartile in England. Assessment of primary-aged pupils is no longer a matter just for the class teacher or the school, due to the pressures of accountability. The different purposes of assessment overlap and are sometimes in conflict with each other. For example, the assessments you do so that you can plan future learning for pupils are not necessarily the assessments that parents or central government want. You would probably find it difficult to plan future lessons for pupils with just a level or grade by their name; you require more information to plan for each pupil's improvement.

Although the statutory requirement for the recording of pupils' achievements is minimal, the reporting of pupil progress to parents is a legal requirement. Each year, a report has to be sent to parents of every pupil in the school. This needs to report on pupils' progress in each subject of the National Curriculum or the EYFSP and include comments on general progress which may include remarks relating to behaviour, attitude and other achievements such as representing the school at football, raising money for a charity or the pupil's peer support of other pupils within the class. At the end of each key stage, you must also provide your assessment results and those gained from pupils' engagement with the end of key stage SATs. You must also provide an opportunity for parents to discuss with you the annual report they receive within two weeks of the parents receiving it. For pupils transferring to secondary school following the summer break, there is a statutory form that also needs to be completed called the Common Transfer File which includes the pupil's unique number, the pupil's educational record and National Curriculum test results.

Similarly, at parents' evenings, you will need to provide evidence of pupil progress through the comments you make, supported by other reports or pupils' work to qualify your comments. It is important when talking with parents to again use the 3:1 principle and avoid using educational jargon or acronyms.

Accountability

Accountability has been evident in education since the 1830s when public money was used to provide a national state education system which led to an inspectorate who monitored the use of the money across the education establishments of the country. In more recent times, accountability was heightened with the first statutory National Curriculum in 1988 and since then there has been a range of systems and structures to ensure teachers and schools are accountable for the public money spent on them which relies largely on quantitative data supplied by schools. Accountability is evident through the use of league tables, Ofsted inspections, performance management and the induction year for newly qualified teachers.

Finally, as a teacher you are accountable because public funds provide your salary. In fact, accountability has moral, legal and financial dimensions (Headington, 2003). You are morally and legally obliged to provide a safe and secure environment in which all pupils can learn and achieve and to provide assessment information to a range of stakeholders. Your first priority is the development of the pupils you teach, providing lessons that are inclusive, challenging and stimulating in which all pupils progress in their learning. Second, you have a legal obligation to report annually to parents and, third, you have a moral and legal obligation to other professionals to provide accurate, relevant and up-to-date information on pupil progress to ensure pupils can be tracked and monitored. Detailed reports on pupil achievement and attainment can then be provided for parents, local authorities and central government. Your ultimate moral and legal responsibility though is to the tax payer, who, in effect, provides your salary and the finances in school that provide resources to support pupil learning. The head teacher and governors have a legal and moral obligation to ensure that the finances the school receives are used effectively in order that pupil outcomes are increased. The governing body is legally responsible for reporting test results to the local authority and the education department of central government. Accountability requires assessment procedures and the results of pupils' assessments to be made publicly available. Similarly, some results, such as the Key Stage 2 SATs, will be placed in league tables, published in Ofsted reports and occasionally reported in the media.

Points for Reflection

- Marking involves assessment, feedback to pupils and a recording of the information.
- Marking should directly relate to the learning objectives.
- Operating 3:1 positive feedback is motivational.
- Using grades, numbers or codes provides limited information on pupil achievements and future learning.
- Recording systems should be effective and efficient and contain carefully selected information that can be used to set targets for pupils, provide the basis of conversations with pupils and reports to other stakeholders such as parents.
- Marking needs to highlight what has been done well and provide information on how to improve. It should feed back and feed forward.
- Feedback should be provided as soon as possible after pupils have completed the tasks.

Further Reading

Connor, C. (1999) *Assessment in Action in the Primary School*. London: Falmer Press.
Drummond, M.J. (2003) *Assessing Children's Learning: Primary*. London: David Fulton.

Gardner, J. (2012) *Assessment and Learning*. London: SAGE.

Gipps, C.V. (1990) *Assessment: A Teacher's Guide to the Issues*. London: Hodder & Stoughton.

Gipps, C.V. (1993) *Beyond Assessment: Towards a Theory of Educational Assessment*. London: Falmer Press.

Johnson, S. (2012) *Assessing Learning in the Primary Classroom*. Abingdon: Routledge.

Slatterley, D. (1989) *Assessment in Schools*. London: Blackwell.

Sutton, R. (1991) *Assessment: A Framework for Teachers*. Abingdon: Routledge.

Torrance, H. and Pryor, J. (1998) *Investigating Formative Assessment: Teaching, Learning and Assessment in the Classroom*. Buckingham: Open University Press.

CONCLUSION

Chapter Objectives

1 To reflect on the main issues raised throughout this book
2 To cause you to reflect on whether the present way in which you
   assess, record and report pupils' achievements could be improved
   to further motivate pupils in their learning

The word assessment is thought to derive from the Latin *ad sedere* which means to sit down beside and was used in the legal profession meaning to reside beside the judge and advise them on legal or technical points. Today, the word assessment in an educational context has a slightly different meaning to that of several years ago, although similarities are evident. The Task Group for Assessment and Testing (1988) suggested assessment was the enhancement of all methods used to appraise and extend the performance of pupils; Headington (2003) refers to it as the work done by teachers to identify the learning needs of pupils; and Walvoord (2010) purports that assessment is the careful use of data to promote learning. Assessment is different from monitoring in so far as monitoring is a passive action to gain an overview of pupils' learning whilst assessment is an action which is focused on one or more pupils in order to identify the learning achieved from which future targets can be set. Assessment also determines the quality of the learning achieved and can be used to ascertain whether this learning will be remembered and, if so, whether it can be applied to other situations. Therefore, assessment is concerned with what, how well and in what way learning has been achieved. Assessment in primary school must thus determine the next steps for pupils to ensure that they will advance in their learning. When assessing pupils, you aim not only to evaluate where they are in their learning but also to advise them on how they can improve. Effective assessment can take place throughout the lesson such as in starters, targeted questions, think-pair-share, traffic lights, use of whiteboards, thumbs up, mind maps, through observations or through mini plenaries to check knowledge, understanding or skills and correct misconceptions.

Teachers have always recorded the outcomes of pupils' work. In the past, this was on slates and in the future there may be an effective digital resource that builds on the ideas discussed in Chapter 10 of this book. At present, there are rudimentary digital means of recording pupil progress but the use of these to record pupil achievement holistically is arguably limited. These types of online assessment tools tend to be summative judgements, often against National Curriculum age-related expectations. Whilst they can plot a pupil's progress against their targets throughout primary school, there is no context placed within this and they tend to be focused on the core subjects of English, maths, science and perhaps ICT. Generally with such online assessments, there is no record of a pupil's development in, for example, artistic flair in gymnastics, their use of perspective in art or their ability to conduct a historical debate. As a tracking mechanism, they are useful but it will be up to you to decide whether such electronic means can provide you with enough information to plan successive lessons that are stimulating, motivational and engaging from which you can assess pupils' learning and set future targets.

Pupils spend a vast amount of time writing but some of this is not read or is purely read to discover what a pupil has done or achieved. Although writing is a very important skill for pupils to master, it does not need to be part of every activity that pupils encounter each day in school. As identified in this book, there are many other ways that you can assess whether a pupil has achieved the learning outcomes of the lesson.

An important point to highlight is that assessment, planning, evaluation and target setting constitute a never-ending cyclical process. They are the ways in which you can address the needs of pupils in your class. You cannot plan effectively without knowing what pupils' targets are and what they already know. You cannot assess without knowing what you want to find out and how you are going to do this. Arguably, you could start at any point in the cyclical process but it is likely that you will start with a basic, simple assessment of where pupils are in their learning. From there, you can set pupil targets and plan your lesson. Once a lesson is complete, you will evaluate it in light of pupils' learning, their attitude to the tasks, their behaviour and how well they achieved the learning outcomes. Of course, the more specific the learning objective, the easier it is to assess pupils. You may choose to adopt a three-tier system of differentiation using words such as: will, should, could. A typical example of this, placed in the context of a lesson, is the following:

- The red group will use seven or more adjectives in their description of the pirate.
- The blue group should use five or more adjectives in their description of the pirate.
- The green group could use at least three adjectives in their description of the pirate.

Being specific should provide you with quality information from which you can plan your next lesson and set new targets for pupils as necessary. As you become a more experienced teacher, this cyclical process will become increasingly automatic. You will become more knowledgeable about the types of assessment that are appropriate within each lesson, how to motivate and engage pupils in their learning and how to set specific, manageable and reasonable targets that are challenging but achievable. Much as with learning to drive a car, or achieve any skill where in the beginning you need to think through all the stages, as you become more proficient these actions will become instinctive.

This book has also explored recording, reporting and accountability. You may excel at planning lessons that are challenging, interesting and fun, weaving assessment through the lesson and setting appropriate targets for pupils, but you must also record the achievements of pupils so that you are able to provide reports for a range of stakeholders. Successive governments since the turn of the twenty-first century have required the profession to become more accountable. Of course, this is correct as the salaries of teachers, many resources and school buildings and land are funded by public money from the tax payer. Accountability in the teaching profession to some degree can be traced back to the mid-nineteenth century but today there is much more focus on culpability as we are firmly responding to globalisation.

There has been an increasing involvement of central government in school since the turn of the twenty-first century in the drive to raise standards (Butt and Gunter, 2007a). The standards of English pupils in reading and writing are regularly pitched against those in the developed world, both with countries that have English as their native tongue and countries with other national languages. The importance of these standards is evident in proposals and policies such as the National Curriculum 2000 (DfEE, 1999) which promised the best possible progress and the maximum attainment for all pupils, and the Importance of Teaching (DfE, 2010b) which stated that the government would ensure England has a world-class school system which our children deserve through re-focusing Ofsted inspections and strengthening the performance measures used to hold schools accountable. The effect of globalisation on the teaching of pupils in English schools is used to evaluate how we are doing compared with our international competitors. Then there are documents such as the Leitch Report (2006) that claim that without an increase in educational standards in England, we will be unable to compete within the top quartile of the world's economy which would lead to diminishing economic growth.

Such focus on the economic prosperity of the country is not aided by publication of the results of international tests such as the Progress in International Reading Literacy Study (PIRLS) (Twist et al., 2001, 2007) which tests the literacy attainment of pupils aged 11. Since 2001, English pupils have seen their attainment being overshadowed by countries such as Bulgaria, Hong Kong and the Russian Federation. Additionally, successive reports indicate that the difference between the highest and lowest performing pupils in England is increasing. In response to this, successive governments have issued a plethora of intervention strategies such as Further Literacy Support (DCSF, 2002) and increased testing, resulting in primary-aged pupils being tested at ages 5, 6, 7 and 11, and 8, 9 and 10, should the school wish to administer the optional tests provided by the government. But there is no evidence to support the fact that more testing improves standards. It may, however, encourage teaching to tests, resulting in pupils not receiving a broad and balanced curriculum. In fact, according to Black and Wiliam (1998), tests encourage rote learning rather than deep and meaningful learning. There is also a flaw in English national tests which is the lack of differentiation of regional and local differences in the school population.

For example, if test papers appeal to pupils in leafy suburb schools in the south of the country, they are probably not appropriate for pupils in inner-city schools in large urban areas such as London, Liverpool, Manchester and Birmingham, as pupils do not have the same life experiences or socio-economic backgrounds. For example, it may be suitable to include study of a Caribbean or African village in one school but, in another school, pupils may have no concept of where these places are because their life experience has not taken them further than the local area. This was illustrated by a pupil who mistook the Pyramids for a shopping centre rather than the ancient Egyptian tombs.

As seen above, assessment of the core subjects in the primary curriculum is set by central government, although, beyond this, with the foundation subjects, assessment largely falls on the individual teacher or more often the individual school. Therefore, it is important that you read a copy of the assessment policy and talk with the assessment coordinator soon after arriving at your school. You will know your pupils better than anyone else, how they can be motivated and to which type of stimuli they best respond. It is also important that you record your assessment results in order to indicate pupil achievements. You need some form of baseline in order to measure the progress of pupils through your assessments. The baseline can be generated from previous assessments of each individual pupil, against the average progress of the class or against age-related expectations of subject-specific levels of the primary curriculum. It is also a good idea to decide when you will do the assessment. Whilst it may seem natural to teach first then assess the learning of pupils, should you choose to assess part way through the lesson or the unit of work then this will provide you with an opportunity to redirect your teaching and allow for misconceptions to be addressed and the pace or direction of the lesson to be changed.

As Chapter 11 explored, you must also find a way to record assessments, which depends on the use which they will serve. Recording at the micro level allows you to remember and recall the significant learning events during each lesson, and analysing these will allow you to set future targets for pupils and plan your next lesson. At a macro level, the assessments you administer with pupils in your class require recording in a different way and for a different purpose. This may be at the end of a unit of work, a national test, to fulfil your statutory duties within this field or in order to report to the senior management team, the governors or parents. It also very much depends on the criteria set for the assessment which should be clearly articulated to pupils. For example, will you be assessing all learning objectives, assessing how pupils work in collaboration or how they can apply their learning to other situations? It is important to remember that decisions on whether to write copious notes or jottings when you record your assessments and how you record these largely fall to you as teacher and often will depend on your confidence and experience, the demands of the day and the activities in which pupils are engaged. The deciding factor is perhaps this: if the senior management team, Ofsted or parents ask you to identify the level at which your pupils are working and their targets, could you provide this information succinctly and accurately? Recording is perhaps more demanding than assessment as it requires you to interpret the results or outcomes of the assessment and use this to plan future lessons. You can of course involve pupils in the recording of their achievements which will aid their reflective skills. This was discussed in earlier chapters with the development of portfolios and e-portfolios (Chapter 9) and the use of mind maps and concept maps (Chapter 7). Alternatively, you can encourage self-reflection and recording through use of thumbs up, smiley faces, traffic lights, target cards or choosing one of three baskets in which to deposit their workbook ('I totally understand', 'I think I understand' or 'I do not understand'). Perhaps the most common form of assessing and recording achievements is self- and peer assessment, which were discussed in Chapter 6.

In conclusion, whilst the assessment of core subjects and reporting procedures are largely set out by central government, you will have a certain level of autonomy in assessing and recording the progress of pupils on a day-to-day and weekly basis. There are perhaps three important points to remember about assessment. First, whatever type of assessment you opt for, it must be worthwhile, manageable and provide information for you to move pupils on in their learning. Second, you cannot divorce assessment from planning and evaluation. They should not be seen as separate components of a lesson but, rather, in your planning, weave assessment through each session. Finally, there is no statutory policy that requires you to assess pupils through written means except for writing and spelling tests. It is right that we should prepare pupils for national tests or exams but assessment should be beneficial for you and the pupil, not for the government, the local authority, the governors, the senior management team or parents.

This book has provided you with knowledge and understanding of the history of assessments and the National Curriculum requirements, but also offered you a range of alternative assessments that may encourage and enthuse pupils to move forward in their learning.

Points for Reflection

- You should access your school's assessment policy as soon as possible to ensure you follow procedures.
- Assessments should be manageable, focused on the learning objectives and used in the future planning of lessons.
- Assessment, planning, evaluation and the setting of targets cannot be separated and form a continuous cyclical pattern.
- Assessment can be carried out in many different ways but should always fit with the learning taking place and offer you valuable data on the learning process and progress achieved.
- Varying the types of assessment you use can motivate pupils in learning, assessing learning and setting future targets for themselves.
- Whilst the assessment of core subjects and the statutory reporting procedures are largely laid out by central government, you have autonomy in how, when and where you assess pupils in other subjects, provided you are able to report progress to various stakeholders if and when required.

REFERENCES

Airasian, P.W. (1991) *Classroom Assessment*. New York: McGraw-Hill.

Alexander, R., Rose, J. and Woodhead, C. (1992) *Curriculum Organisation and Classroom Practice in Primary Schools*. London: Crown.

Andrew-Power, K. and Gormley, C. (2009) *Display for Learning*. London: Network Continuum.

Assessment of Performance Unit (2008) The Assessment of Performance Unit: its task and rationale. London: DES.

Assessment Reform Group (2002a) *Assessment for Learning: 10 Principles*. Cambridge: ARG.

Assessment Reform Group (2002b) *Testing, Motivation and Learning*. Cambridge: Cambridge University Press.

Assessment Reform Group (2002c) *Research-based Principles to Guide Classroom Practice*. London: Nuffield Foundation.

Assessment Reform Group (2003) *The Role of Teachers in the Assessment of Learning*. London: Nuffield Foundation.

Assessment Reform Group (2008) *Changing Assessment Practice: Process, Principles and Standards*. London: Nuffield Foundation.

Association for Achievement and Improvement through Assessment (AAIA) (2005) *Managing Assessment for Learning*. London: AAIA.

Association of Teachers and Lecturers (ATL) (2003) *Right From the Start: Early Years Education and Practice*. London: ATL.

Augar, N., Raitman, R. and Zhou, Q. (2004) 'Teaching and Learning Online with Wikis'. *School of Information Technology*, Deakin University.

Axel, B. and Humphreys, S. (2005) *Wikis in Teaching and Assessment*. The M/Cyclopedia Project, San Diego, CA.

Ball, S. (2008) *The Education Debate*. Bristol: The Policy Press.

Ball, S., Goodson, I.F. and Maguire, M. (2007) *Education, Globalisation and New Times*. Abingdon: Routledge.

Barber, D. and Cooper, L. (2012) *Using New Web Tools in the Primary Classroom: A Practical Guide for Enhancing Teaching and Learning*. Abingdon: Routlege.

Bates, J., Lewis, S. and Pickard, A. (2011) *Education Policy, Practice and the Professional*. London: Continuum.

Beauchamp, G. (2012) *ICT in the Primary School: From Pedagogy to Practice*. Harlow: Pearson Education.

Black, P. (1998) *Testing: Friend or Foe? Theory and Practice of Assessment and Testing*. London: Falmer Press.

Black, P. and Wiliam, D. (1998) *Inside the Black Box: Raising Standards Through Classroom Assessment*. London: Phi Delta Kappa International.

Black, P. and Wiliam, D. (2002) *Assessment for Learning: Putting It Into Practice*. London: McGraw-Hill.

Black, P. and Wiliam, D. (2008) 'Assessment for Learning in the Classroom', in J. Gardner (ed.), *Assessment for Learning*. London: SAGE.

Black, P., Harrison, C., Lee, C., Bethan, M., Marshall, B. and Wiliam, D. (2002) *Working Inside the Black Box*. London: Open University Press.

Black, P., Harrison, C., Lee, C., Bethan, M., Marshall, B. and Wiliam, D. (2003a) *Assessment for Learning: Putting it into Practice*. London: Open University Press.

Black, P., Wiliam, D., Lee, C. and Harrison, C. (2003b) *Teachers Developing Assessment for Learning: Impact on Student Achievement*. London: Taylor & Francis.

Bloom, B.S. and Krathwohl, D.R. (1956) 'Taxonomy of Educational Objectives: The classification of Educational Goals'. In *Committee of College and University Examiners. Handbook 1: Cognitive Domain*. New York: Longman.

Bowden, J. (2008) *Writing a Report: How to Prepare, Write and Present Really Effective Reports*. Oxford: How To Books.

Broadfoot, P. (2007) *An Introduction to Assessment*. London: Continuum.

Brown, S., Race, P. and Smith, B. (1996) *500 Tips on Assessment*. London: Kogan Page.

Bruner, J.S. (1957) On perceptual readiness, *Psychological Review*, 64 (2): 123–152.

Burden, R. (1998) 'Assessing Children's Perceptions of Themselves as Learners and Problem Solvers. The construction of the Myself-as-a-Learner Scale (MALS)', *School Psychology International*, 19: 291–305.

Butler, R.A. (1944) 'The 1944 Education Act'. London: HC Deb, 19 January, Vol. 396 cc207–322. Available at: http://hansard.millbanksystems.com (accessed 11/02/11).

Butt, G. (2010) *Making Assessment Matter*. London: Continuum.

Butt, G. and Gunter, H. (2007a) *Modernizing Schools*. London: Continuum.

Butt, G. and Gunter, H. (2007b) 'Remodelling Learning: The Use of Technology', in G. Butt and H. Gunter (eds), *Modernizing Schools: People, Learning and Organization*. London: Continuum.

Butt, G. and Lance, A. (2005) 'Modernizing the Roles of Support Staff in Primary Schools: Changing Focus, Changing Function', *Educational Reviewer*, 57(2): 139–49.

Buzan, T. (2004) *Mind Maps at Work: How to be the Best at Your Job and Still Have the Time to Play*. London: Bath Press.

Buzan, T. and Buzan, B. (2003) *The Mind Map Book*. London: BBC Worldwide.

Carr, M. (2001) *Assessment in Early Childhood Settings: Learning Stories*. London: Paul Chapman.

Carr, M. (2004) *Assessment for Learning: Early Childhood Examples*. Wellington, NZ: Ministry of Education.

Chitty, C. (2009) *Education Policy in Britain*. Basingstoke: Macmillan.

Clarke, S. (1998) *Targeting Assessment in the Primary Classroom*. London: Hodder & Stoughton.

Clarke, S. (2001) *Unlocking Formative Assessment: Practical Strategies for Enhancing Pupils' Learning in the Primary Classroom*. London: Hodder & Stoughton.

Clarke, S. (2005a) *The Power of Formative Assessment*. London: Hodder & Stoughton.

Clarke, S. (2005b) *Formative Assessment in Action: Weaving the Elements Together*. London: Hodder Education.

Clarke, S. (2008) *Active Learning through Formative Assessment*. London: Hodder & Stoughton.

Clough, P. (1998) *Managing Inclusive Education: From Policy to Experience*. London: SAGE.

Cowie, B. and Bell, B. (1999) 'A Model of Formative Assessment in Science Education', *Assessment in Education*, 6: 101–7.

Crocker, A.C. and Cheeseman, R.G. (1988) 'The Ability of Young Children to Rank Themselves for Academic Ability', *Education Studies*, 14(1): 105–10.

Crooks, T.J. (1988) 'The Impact of Classroom Evaluation Practices on Students', *Review of Educational Research*, 58(4): 438–81.

Crooks, T. (2001) 'The Validity of Formative Assessments', British Educational Research Association Conference, Leeds, September.

Dale, R. (1981) *From Expectations to Outcomes in Educational Systems*. Milton Keynes: Open University Press.

D'Antoni, A. (2006) 'Applications of the Mind Map Learning Technique in Chiropractic Education: A Pilot Study and Literature Review', *Journal of Chiropractic Humanities*, 9(2): 111–20.

D'Antoni, A., Pinto Zipp, G., Olson, V.G. and Cahill, T.F. (2010) 'Does the Mind Map Learning Strategy Facilitate Information Retrieval and Critical Thinking in Medical Students?', *Medical Education*, 10(61).

Darling-Hammond, L., Ancess, J. and Falk, B. (1995) *Authentic Assessment in Action Studies of Schools and Students at Work*. New York: Teachers' College Press.

Dearing, R. (1994) *The National Curriculum and its Assessment: Final Report*. London: SCAA.

De Bono, E. (1995) 'Serious Creativity', *The Journal for Quality and Participation*, 18(12).

De Mestral, F. (1955) G DE – US Patent 2,717,437

Department for Children, Schools and Families (DCSF) (2004) *The Primary National Strategy: Excellence and Enjoyment – Learning and Teaching in the Primary Years*. London: DCSF.

Department for Children, Schools and Families (DCSF) (2007) *The Children's Plan. Building Brighter Futures*. London: Crown.

Department for Children, Schools and Families (DCSF) (2008) *The Assessment for Learning Strategy*. London: DCSF.

Department for Education (DfE) (2010a) *Reading by Six: How the Best Schools Do It*. London: Crown.

Department for Education (DfE) (2010b) *The Importance of Teaching: The Schools White Paper 2010*. London: HMSO.

Department for Education (2011) *Supporting Aspiration: A New Approach to Special Educational Needs and Disability*. London: Crown.

Department for Education (DfE) (2012) *Statutory Framework for the Early Years Foundation Stage* (EYFS). London: Crown.

Department for Education (DfE) (2013) *About the P Scales*. Available at: www.education.gov.uk

Department for Education (DfE) (2014) *The Primary National Curriculum*. London: HMSO.

Department for Education and Employment (DfEE) (1966) *Desirable Outcomes for Children's Learning on Entering Compulsory Education*. London: SCAA.

Department for Education and Employment (DfEE) (1997) *Excellence for all Pupils: Meeting the Needs of Pupils with Special Educational Needs*. London: HMSO.

Department for Education and Employment (DfEE) (1999) *The National Curriculum 2000*. London: HMSO.

Department for Education and Employment (DfEE) (2001) *The Special Educational Needs Code of Practice*. London: HMSO.

Department for Education and Skills (DfES) (1988) *The National Curriculum*. London: HMSO.

Department for Education and Skills. (2002) *Further Literacy Support*. London: Crown.

Department for Education and Skills (DfES) (2003) *Birth to Three Matters*. London: Crown.

Department for Education and Skills (DfES) (2005) *Social and Emotional Aspects of Learning (SEAL)*. London: Crown.

Department for Education and Skills (DfES) (2006) *The Children's Act*. Annesley: Crown.

Department of Education and Science (DES) (1988) *Education Reform Act*. London: HMSO.

Dix, P. (2010) *The Essential Guide to Classroom Assessment*. Harlow: Pearson.

Docking, J. (2000) *New Labour's Policies for Schools*. London: David Fulton.

Drake, J. (2005) *Planning Children's Play and Learning in the Foundation Stage*. London: David Fulton.

Drummond, M.J. (1999) 'Baseline Assessment: A Case for Civil Disobedience', in C. Conner (ed.), *Assessment in Action in the Primary School*. London: Falmer Press.

Drummond, M.J. (2003) *Assessing Children's Learning*. London: David Fulton.

Dyrud, M.A., Worley, R.B. and Flatley, M.E. (2005) 'Blogging for Enhanced Teaching and Learning', *Business Communication Quarterly*, 68(1): 77–80.

Edgington, M. (2004) *The Foundation Stage Teacher in Action: Teaching 3, 4 and 5 Year Olds*. London: Paul Chapman.

Elbaum, B., and Vaughn, S. (2001) 'School Based Interventions to Enhance the Self-Concept of Students with Learning Disabilities: a Meta-Analysis', *Elementary School Journal*, 101(3): 303–29.

Elmore, R.F. (1989) 'Backward Mapping: Implementation Research and Policy Decisions', in B. Moon, P. Murphy and J. Rayner (eds), *Policies for the Curriculum*. London: Hodder & Stoughton.

Eppler, M.J. (2006) 'A Comparison Between Concept Maps, Mind Maps, Conceptual Diagrams and Visual Metaphors as Complementary Tools for Knowledge Construction and Sharing', *Information Visualisation*, 5: 202–10.

Farrand, P., Hussain, F. and Hennessy, E. (2002) 'The Efficacy of the Mind Map Study Technique', *Medical Education*, 36: 426–31.

Farrell, M. (2004) *Special Educational Needs: A Resource for Practitioners*. London: Paul Chapman.

Fautley, M. and Savage, M. (2008) *Achieving QTS: Meeting the Professional Standards Framework – Assessment for Learning and Teaching in Secondary Schools*. Exeter: Learning Matters.

Frith, U. (1999) 'Paradoxes in the Definition of Dyslexia', *Dyslexia*, 5(4): 192–214.

Gardner, H. (2006) *Changing Minds: The Art and Science of Changing our Own and Other People's Minds*. Boston: Harvard Business School Press.

Gibson, A. and Asthana, S. (1999) 'Schools, Markets and Equity: Access to Secondary Education in England and Wales'. Paper presented to the American Education Association Annual Conference, Montreal, Canada, 21 April.

Giddens, A. (1996) *Introduction to Sociology*. New York: W.W. Norton.

Gilbert, F. (2012) 'Is Coursework a Fair Way of Assessing Pupils?', *The Times*, 8 May.

Gillard, D. (2011) *Education in England: A Brief History*. Available at: www. educationengland.org.uk (accessed 10/02/11).

Gipps, C. (1994) *Beyond Testing*. Lewes: Falmer Press.

Gipps, C. and Goldstein, H. (1983) *Monitoring Children: An Evaluation of the Assessment of Performance Unit*. London: Heinemann.

Goldstein, H. and Lewis, H. (1996) *Assessment: Problems, Developments and Statistical Issues*. London: Wiley.

Guerney, P. (1987) 'Self-esteem Enhancement in Children: A Review of Research Findings', *Educational Research*, 29(2): 130–6.

Gunter, H. (2007) 'Remodelling the School Workforce in England: A Study in Tyranny', *Journal for Critical Education Policy Studies*, 5(1): 1–15.

Hammersley, B. (2004) 'Audible Revolution', *The Guardian Online*. Available at: www.guardian.co.uk

Hatcher, R. (2001) 'Getting Down to Business: Schooling in the Globalised Economy', *Education and Social Justice*, 3(2): 45–59.

Hay, D.B. and Kinchin, I.M. (2006) 'Using Concept Maps to Reveal Conceptual Typologies', *Education and Training*, 48(2/3): 127–42.

Headington, R. (2003) *Monitoring, Assessment, Recording, Reporting and Accountability*. Abingdon: David Fulton.

Hebert, E.A. (2001) *The Power of Portfolios: What Children Can Teach Us About Learning and Assessment*. San Francisco: Jossey-Bass.

Hufflaker, D. (2004) 'The Educated Blogger: Using Weblogs to Promote Literacy in the Classroom', *First Monday*, 9(6): 1–6.

Humphrey, N. (2002) 'Teacher and Pupil Ratings of Self-esteem in Developmental Dyslexia', *British Journal of Special Education*, 2(1): 29–36.

Hutchin, V. (2012) *Assessing and Supporting Young Children's Learning*. Abingdon: Hodder.

Jessop, B. (2002) *The Future of the Capitalist State*. Cambridge: Polity Press.

Johnson, S. (2011) *Assessing Learning in the Primary Classroom*. London: Routledge.

Johnson, S. (2012) *Assessing Learning in the Classroom*. Abingdon: Routledge.

Karge, B. (2006) 'Knowing What to Teach: Using Authentic Assessment to Improve Classroom Instruction', *Reading and Writing Quarterly: Overcoming Learning Difficulties*, 14: 319–31.

Kickert, W. (1991) 'Steering at a Distance: A New Paradigm of Public Governance in Dutch Higher Education'. Paper presented to the European Consortium for Political Research, University of Essex.

Klenowski, V. (2002) *Developing Portfolios for Learning and Assessment*. London: RoutledgeFalmer.

Lawton, D. (1994) *The Tory Mind on Education 1979–94*. London: Falmer Smith.

Leitch, S. (2006) The Leitch Review of Skills: Prosperity for all in the global economy – world class skills. Executive Summary and Foreword. Norwich: HMSO.

Lepper, M.R. and Hodell, M. (1989) 'Intrinsic Motivation in the Classroom', in C. Ames and R. Ames (eds), *Research on Motivation in Education*. San Diego: Academic Press.

Leuf, B. and Cunningham, W. (2001) *The Wiki Way: Quick Collaboration on the Web*. Boston: Addison Wesley.

Lieberman, L.J. and Houston-Wilson, C. (2002) *Strategies for Inclusion: A Handbook for Physical Educators*. Leeds: Human Kinetics.

Linnenbrink, E.A. and Pintrich, P.R. (2003) 'The Role of Self-efficacy Beliefs in Student Engagement and Learning in the Classroom', *Reading & Writing Quarterly*, 19(2): 119–37.

Littleboy, L., Reed, M. and Thompson, J. (2000) *Special Educational Needs in Early Years Care and Education*. London: Harcourt.

Lowe, M. and Hammersley-Fletcher, L. (2009) *From General Dogsbody to Whole Class Delivery: the Role of Teaching Assistants in the Education of pupils in England*, Working Paper.

Maslow, A. (1943) *Hierarchy of Needs*. http://psychology.about.com [accessed 12/02/11].

McLeod, R. (ed.) (1982) *Days of Judgement: Science Examinations and the Organisation of Knowledge in Late Victorian England*. Driffield: Nafferton Books.

Mento, A.J., Martinelli, P. and Jones, R.M. (1999) 'Mind Mapping in Executive Education: Applications and Outcomes', *Journal of Management Development*, 18(4): 390–407.

Mindes, G. (2011) *Assessing Young Children*. Hoboken, NJ: Pearson.

Moon, J.A. (1999) *Learning Journals: A Handbook for Academics, Students and Professional Development*. London: Kogan Page.

Moon, J.A. (2006) *Learning Journals: A Handbook for Reflective Practice and Professional Development*. Abingdon: Routledge.

Morrow, R.A. and Torres, C.A. (2000) 'The State, Globalisation and Educational Policy', in N.C. Burbules and C.A. Torres (eds), *Globalisation and Education: Critical Perspectives*. New York: Routledge.

Moser, C. (1999) *Report Summary and Recommendations*. London: Department for Education and Skills.

Mosley, J. (2006) *Step-by-Step Guide to Circle Time for SEAL*. Trowbridge: Positive Press.

Nast, J. (2006) *Idea Mapping*. Hoboken, NJ: John Wiley & Sons.

Office for Standards in Education (Ofsted) (1996) *The Framework for the Inspection of Schools*. London: Ofsted.

Office for Standards in Education (Ofsted) (2008a) *Assessment for Learning: The Impact of National Strategy Support*. London: Ofsted.

Office for Standards in Education (Ofsted) (2010) *The Special Educational Needs and Disability Review: A Statement is Not Enough*. Manchester: Crown.

Organisation for Economic Cooperation and Development (OECD) (2000) PISA Study. UNICEF Report. Available at: www.members.cox.net (accessed 27/03/08).

Organisation for Economic Cooperation and Development (OECD) (2006) PISA Study. UNICEF Report. Available at: www.members.cox.net (accessed 27/03/08).

Organisation for Economic Cooperation and Development (OECD) (2009) PISA Study. UNICEF Report. Available at: www.members.cox.net (accessed 27/03/08).

Ormond, P.R. (2008) *Podcasting Enhances Learning*. Orem, UT: Consortium for Computing Science in Colleges.

Palloff, R.M. and Pratt, K. (1999) *Building Learning Communities in Cyberspace*. San Francisco: Jossey-Bass.

Pardoe, D. (2009) *Towards Successful Learning*. London: Bloomsbury.

Peer, L. and Reid, G. (2003) *Introduction to Dyslexia*. London: David Fulton Publishers.

Piaget, J. (1936) *The Origins of Intelligence in Children*. New York: International Universities Press.

Pidmore, V.N. and Luff, P. (2012) *Observation: Origins and Approaches in Early Childhood*. Maidenhead: Open University Press.

Plowden, B. (1967) *Plowden Report: Children and their Primary Schools*. London: HMSO.

Popham, J. (1987) 'The Merits of Measurement-Driven Instruction', *Phi Delta Kappa*, pp. 679–82.

Pring, R. (1996) 'Standards and Quality in Education', in A. Craft (ed.), *Primary Education: Assessing and Planning Learning*. London: Routledge.

Progoff, I. (1975) *At a Journal Workshop*. New York: Dialogue House Library.

Qualifications and Curriculum Authority (QCA) (2001) *What are 'P' Scales?* London: BBC Active.

Qualifications and Curriculum Authority (QCA) (2005a) *The P Scales: English, Mathematics and Science Level Descriptors P1 to P8*. London: QCA.

Raynor, S. (2007) *Managing Special and Inclusive Education*. London: SAGE.

Reid, G. (2005) *Dyslexia*. London: Continuum International Publishing Group.

Rega, B. (1993) 'Fostering Creativity in Advertising Students: Incorporating the Theories of Multiple Intelligences and Integrative Learning'. Annual Meeting of the Association for Education in Journalism and Mass Communication, Washington.

Richardson, W. (2009) *Blogs, Wikis, Podcasts and Other Powerful Web Tools for Classrooms*. London: SAGE.

Rizvi, F. and Lingard, B. (2010) *Globalising Education Policy*. Abingdon: Routledge.

Ross, M., Radnor, H., Mitchell, S. and Bierton, C. (1993) *Assessing Achievement in the Arts*. Buckingham: Open University Press.

Rubie-Davies, C. M., Blatchford, P., Webster, R., Koutsoubou, M. and Bassett, P. (2010) 'Enhancing Learning? A Comparison of Teacher and Teaching Assistant Interactions with Pupils'. School Effectiveness and School Improvement, 21(4): 429–49.

Rynne, E. (2009) 'What are the Challenges of E-assessment?', in P. Wheeden and G. Utt (eds), *Assessing Progress in Your Key Stage Geography Curriculum*. Sheffield: Geographical Association.

Sainsbury, M. (2004) *Making Sense of Baseline Assessment*. Abingdon: Bookprint.

Schwartz, L., Clark, S., Cossarin, M. and Rudolph, J. (2004) 'Technical Evaluation Report 27. Educational Wikis: Features and Selection Criteria', *The International Review of Research in Open and Distance Learning*, 5(1): 1–4.

Scott, R. (2004) *Dyslexia and Counselling*. London: Whurr.

Sellman, E. (2012) *Creative Learning for Inclusion: Creative Approaches to Meet Special Needs in the Classroom*. Abingdon: Routledge.

Shaw, M. (2009) 'A Week in Education', *Times Educational Supplement News*, 16 January. Available at: www.tes.co.uk (accessed 12/08/09).

Shorrocks-Taylor, D. (1999) *National Testing: Past, Present and Future*. Leicester: British Psychological Society.

Siraj-Blatchford, I., Sylva, K., Melhuish, E. and Sammons, P. (2004) *The Effective Provision of Pre-School Education (EPPE) Project: Final Report – A Longitudinal Study Funded by the DfES 1997–2004*. London: Crown.

Smith, M.L. (1991) 'Put to the Test: The Effects of External Testing on Teachers', *Educational Researcher*, 25(5): 8–11.

Spring, J. (2009) *Globalisation of Education*. Abingdon: Routledge.

Standards and Testing Agency (STA) (2013) *Key Stage 1 Assessment and Reporting Arrangements*. London: Crown.

Stefani, L., Mason, R. and Pegler, C. (2007) *The Educational Potential of E-portfolios: Supporting Personal Development and Reflective Learning*. Abingdon: Routledge.

Sterling, C.M. and Robson, C. (eds) (1992) *Psychology, Spelling and Education*. Bristol: Multilingual Matters.

Task Group for Assessment and Testing (TGAT) (1987) *National Curriculum: Task Group on Assessment and Testing – A Report*. London: DES.

Taylor, T. (1977) *The Taylor Report: A New Partnership for Our Schools*. London: HMSO.

Thane, P. (2011) 'The History of Early Years Child Care'. A discussion paper based on a presentation at the Department for Education, 6 October.

Thornton, M. and Hedges, C. (2006) The Active Engagement of Teaching Assistants in Teaching and Learning. National Teacher Research Panel for the Teacher Research Conference 2006. DfES: NTRP.

Tickell, C. (2011) *The Tickell Report*. London: Crown.

Tomlinson, S. (2005) *Education in a Post-Welfare Society*. Buckingham: Open University Press.

Topping, K. and Malony, S. (eds) (2005) *The RoutledgeFalmer Reader in Inclusive Education*. Abingdon: Routledge.

Torrance, H. and Pryor, J (1998) *Investigating Formative Assessment*. Buckingham: Open University Press.

Twist, L., Sainsbury, M., Woodthorpe, A. and Whetton, C. (2001) *Progress in International Reading Literacy Study (PIRLS): Reading All Over the World*. Slough: National Foundation for Educational Research.

Twist, L., Schagen, I. and Hodgson, C. (2007) *Progress in International Reading Literacy Study (PIRLS): Readers and Reading. National Report for England*. Slough: National Foundation for Educational Research.

Vincett, K., Cremin, H. and Thomas, G. (2005) *Teachers & Assistants Working Together*. Berkshire: Open University Press.

Van Ments, M. (1983) *The Effective Use of Role Play: A Handbook for Teachers and Trainers*. London: Kogan Page.

Vygotsky, L.S. (1978) *Mind in Society*. Cambridge, MA: Harvard University Press.

Waddell, J. (1978) *The Waddell Report: School Examinations*. London: HMSO.

Walvoord, B. (2010). *Assessment Clear and Simple: A Practical Guide for Institutions, Departments and General Education*. San Francisco: John Wiley & Sons.

Wales, J (2001) Founder of Wikipedia

Wandersee, J. (1990) 'The Concept Map as a Research Tool: Exploring Conceptual Change in Biology', *Journal of Research in Science Teaching*, 27: 1033–52.

Ward, S. and Eden, C. (2009) *Key Issues in Education Policy*. London: SAGE.

Warnock, H.M. (1978) *The Warnock Report: Special Educational Needs*. London: Crown.

Weeden, P., Winter, J. and Broadfoot, P. (2002) *Assessment: What's in it for Schools?* Abingdon: Routledge.

Westbrook, S.L. (1998) 'Examining the Conceptual Organization of Students in an Integrated Algebra and Physical Science Class', *School Science and Mathematics*, 98: 84–92.

Westwood, P. (2007) *Common-Sense Methods for Children with Special Educational Needs*. London: Routledge.

White, J. (2008) *The Aims of School Education*. Available at: http://www.ippr.org (accessed 13/12/10).

Wolf, A. (1994) *Criterion-Referenced Assessment*. Buckingham: Open University Press.

Wolfendale, S. (ed.) (1994) *Assessing Special Educational Needs*. London: Cassell.

Woods, J., Hammersley-Fletcher, L. and Cole, M. (2009) *Teaching Assistants in Schools – Some Reflections on their Changing Roles*, BERA Conference 3rd – 6th September 2009 Working Paper.

Wragg, E.C. (2001) *Assessment and Learning in the Primary School*. London: Routledge.

Wragg, E.C. and Brown, G. (2001) *Questioning in the Primary School*. London: RoutledgeFalmer.

Wright, R.J. (2010) *Multifaceted Assessment for Early Childhood Education*. London: SAGE.

Young, T. (2010) 'British School Children Now Ranked 23rd in the World, Down From 12th in 2000', *The Telegraph*, 7 December.

Zajda, J. and Rust, V. (eds) (2009) *Globalisation, Policy and Comparative Research: Discourses of Globalisation*. Milton Keynes: Springer.

INDEX